NAVIGATING
CAREER
NEGOTIATIONS
How to Avoid A Lifetime of Getting Less Than You Deserve

HOWARD MATALON & HEATHER MATALON

——————— A NAV™ PUBLICATION ———————

Copyright © 2023 by Negotiations Accelerating Value LLC (NAV™)

All rights reserved. This book or any portion thereof may not be reproduced or used in any manner whatsoever without the express written permission of the publisher except for the use of brief quotations in a book review.

Printed in the United States of America

First Printing, 2023
ISBN 979-8-9884080-1-7

Negotiations Accelerating Value LLC (NAV)
141 Post Kennel Road
Far Hills, New Jersey 07931
navscoring.com

This book is dedicated to the world's extraordinary career professionals, those who work tirelessly to make a difference in the lives of others and the businesses they indispensably serve.

CONTENTS

Preface	1
REALIZING THE TRUE POTENTIAL OF OUR CAREERS	
Introduction	7
NEGOTIATE SMARTER AND AVOID MILLION-DOLLAR MISTAKES	
Chapter One	9
ARE YOU BUYING OR SELLING WHEN IT COMES TO EMPLOYMENT OPPORTUNITIES?	
You Are the Asset	12
If You Are the Seller, What Are You Selling Anyway?	12
Sizing Up Negotiations Correctly Leads to an Amazing Revelation	14
Understanding Your Leverage	15
Chapter Two	21
WHAT ARE YOU REALLY NEGOTIATING FOR (BEYOND THE MONEY)?	
Indefinite Plans	22
Certain Futures	23
Chapter Three	27
DO YOU ACTUALLY KNOW WHO YOU ARE GOING TO WORK FOR?	
Trust but Verify	28
Read the Signs	30
Assess the Sticking Points	32
Know When to Walk Away, Know When to Run	32
Gut Reactions Really Matter: Four Paradigms	33

Chapter Four — 39

WHY IS FOCUSING ON SALARY THE WORST WAY TO NEGOTIATE TERMS OF EMPLOYMENT?

The Crown Jewel of All Employment Offers Is an *Intangible:* Role	42
Employers Will Negotiate Almost Anything	43
Why We Often Negotiate Roles Poorly	45
Three Case Studies of Role Impact on Compensation	49
Opportunity Costs: The Most Overlooked Variable	51
Now We Can Talk About Compensation	52
Watch Your Step: The Pitfalls in Employment Agreements	53

Chapter Five — 57

WHY IS SHARING YOUR SALARY INFORMATION SO DAMAGING TO YOUR CAREER?

Selling Ourselves Short	57
Turning the Tables	59

Chapter Six — 61

SHOULD YOU STAY OR SHOULD YOU GO?

Time Cuts Both Ways	62
Age Is Not the Problem	64
Experiencing Job Decay	65
Factors Impacting the Rate of Job Decay	72
Managing Your Trajectory	77
Race to the C-Suite	80
Attracting New Talent by Any Means Necessary	83
You Are Not the Only Party Assessing Value	84
Getting Ahead Rather than Lagging Behind Is a Must	85

Chapter Seven   89
SHOULD YOU TAKE IT OR LEAVE IT?
Fixing the Problem Requires Another Critical Mindset Shift	91
You Trade Away Value Every Time You Bet Against Yourself	93

Chapter Eight   99
ARE THERE WAYS TO PROTECT YOURSELF FROM GETTING FIRED?
Documentation Is Your Best Friend	100
Lock in Your Severance Package	102
Include Good Reason Clauses	105
Negotiate Equity Acceleration	106

Chapter Nine   109
CAN YOU NEGOTIATE YOUR OWN DEPARTURE WITH SEVERANCE?
Lack of Severance Agreement Is Not Fatal to Separation Payments	110
Resignations Can Come with Payouts	111

Chapter Ten   117
DO CAREER COACHES REALLY MAKE A DIFFERENCE IN EMPLOYMENT OPPORTUNITIES?
Repositioning	120
Knowledge	120
Time	120
Perspective and Objectivity	121
Preventative Maintenance	122
Confidentiality	122

CONCLUSION	125
CAREER EXERCISES	128
GLOSSARY	138
ACKNOWLEDGMENTS	144
AUTHOR BIOS	147

PREFACE

REALIZING THE TRUE POTENTIAL OF OUR CAREERS

"Don't compromise yourself. You are all you've got."

Janis Joplin

What if you could make $1.5 million more over the course of your career just by recognizing your true value and negotiating better on your own behalf? Does it surprise you to learn that every minute of the day, even the smartest career professionals are trading away their value and have only a mere inkling that it is happening to them?

Unfortunately, they are in good company. The problem is so pervasive that it is affecting career climbers at almost every level. Heather and I have had front-row seats to the tragic consequences of this phenomenon, devoting our working lives to understanding the significance and meaning of the career journeys of others. For my part, over the past thirty-plus years, I have had the incredible opportunity as an employment attorney to represent employers in all aspects of the employee lifecycle (more on that later) and to represent employees in their hiring and separation negotiations over a wide variety of industries. Heather has an MBA and has spent her career working in brand management and marketing, mainly for Fortune 500 consumer packaged goods companies. Over the course of our careers, our friends and family and the stream of clients in my employment law practice have given us more than an earful of complaints about their jobs. While the stories are all unique, the problems are troubling, repetitive, and, most importantly, largely preventable.

Some of the most sophisticated, seasoned, and well-educated professionals we knew were not advocating for themselves in ways that helped them maximize their career journey. Whether emerging in their careers or already leading experts in their industries, they consistently settled for less by failing to appreciate or assert their true value in employment negotiations. We witnessed the fear and trepidation with which many approached the hiring process and took note of their feelings of intimidation, deference, and insecurity. As our four daughters began to reach employment age, we observed that they quickly developed the same erroneous thinking.

But it was not just in the context of a new job that we saw these troubling dynamics. These consummate professionals were being undervalued in their current positions but were reluctant to make a change because of the anxiety and uncertainty that comes with changing jobs. They would not even change when it was clear they could not keep their careers on track because the advancement, skill expansion, and experience needed to benefit their careers was unavailable to them where they were still working.

While women experience this phenomenon of "settling for less" far more acutely than men, it is not a gender-specific issue. The employment process intimidates men and women differently but in very fundamental ways, whether it is searching, interviewing, or negotiating a position or the anxiety that comes with leaving a job with known issues for the uncertain landscape of a new one. These overarching concerns invariably led many of our colleagues to remain in positions with little or no value to them, or worse, taking new roles that did not serve their best interests. We affectionately refer to this cycle as the doom loop.

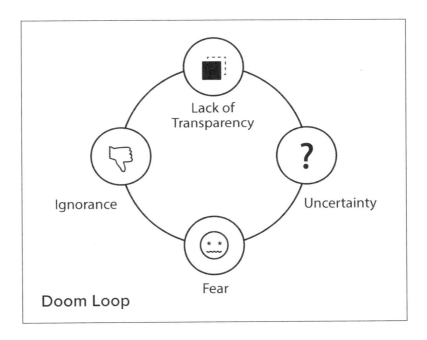

The outcome in each of these situations was always the same: dissatisfaction by employers and employees alike that played out in an endless and seemingly unbreakable cycle because of conditions they did not know how to resolve. Heather and I, who are both entrepreneurs at heart (shoutout to the Entrepreneurs' Organization for that experiential development), saw this problem as an incredible call to action. An opportunity to develop a transformative process in the employment space by educating and empowering motivated professionals to replace their fear, uncertainty, and doubt with concrete fact and analysis. Specifically, we wanted to create a more meaningful negotiation process by providing a deeper understanding of how employers think and giving professionals greater insight into their own value.

Our aspiration to create new tools around these principles quickly led us to the realization that building or improving employment situations required unique insight that had nothing to do with legal work. By the time professionals were contacting attorneys, many of them had already veered off track and had compromised relationships with current or prospective employers. It was not legal guidance that they needed; employment law just dictates the rules of employment the way sports regulations dictate the rules needed to play the game. What professionals *really* needed to understand is how to make the plays themselves.

At Heather's suggestion, I rounded out my legal work as an attorney with human resources and coaching training at Cornell University, where she obtained her MBA from The Johnson Graduate School of Management. This training helped us realize that there was more impactful work to do. We needed to help professionals learn how to negotiate for value rather than just telling them the legal terms and conditions of their employment agreements. In fact, without the right advice in that space, professionals were not recognizing their value and were trading it away. In the years that followed, as we put this revised thinking into practice, we began to realize the massive scope of the problem.

Whether it is simply nature or learned conditioning, human beings are often poor judges of their value in the workplace. As a result, they wind up or remain in roles for which they are underutilized, overqualified, poorly compensated, or all of the above. What ultimately follows from these terrible situations are dissatisfied employees whose talents are poorly utilized, who flounder in great job markets, and ultimately leave positions in frustration. This mindset can put careers in an "off track" position, with hard-to-explain gaps or flagging performance in subsequent roles because they never obtained jobs that positioned them for success. The flipside to this problem is unhappy employers who now need to locate and replace those employees at added cost. Both sides have lost precious time and money in a completely avoidable situation.

One critical takeaway from our assessment is that many employees are failing themselves badly in the negotiation process. They are not sizing up their roles properly. They are not getting the compensation they deserve. They are missing the hidden **opportunity costs** limiting the growth and advancement that comes with every opportunity. In short, employees are consistently ignoring fundamental issues because of a lack of insight and because of the fear, uncertainty, and doubt that clouds judgment and impairs confidence. The lack of guidance in this space led to stale positions, declining performance, and ultimately employees walking out the door.

So, what we really needed to make impactful differences in employment situations was to:

- Figure out why the existing system consistently failed professionals.
- Build and develop a non-legal, practical assessment tool that properly framed who the parties are, explained how they correlated with one another, and coached them on how to better negotiate opportunities to maximize their career value.

This assessment tool would lead to better alignment, improved retention, and greater **return on investment (ROI)** for both sides.

The results of our developing and using this tool were astounding, and we knew we needed to share this insight with as broad an audience as possible to elicit real change in the employment dynamic. While results varied in impact, in every situation where we put this assessment tool to use, professionals had immediate gains in understanding and were able to improve the value of current and prospective job opportunities.

By focusing our work on the employee side of things, we were helping them navigate careers through knowledge and action, realizing future goals, and improving career trajectories. We also came to the realization that professionals need someone to coach them through the entire employment lifecycle and to help them understand that they deserved – and could no doubt receive – a far better employment package than they were prepared to accept. This formative thinking became the blueprint for a system to optimize career growth and development and, as we discuss in the last chapter of this book, the foundation of our own groundbreaking business in this space.

We knew we could do more to help career climbers break a seemingly endless cycle of oversights and miscalculations, and this drive served as our stimulus for this book. We do not want anyone else to fear change, suffer needlessly, or undervalue themselves any longer. It is time to redress the balance and empower motivated career professionals everywhere.

We now share that thinking with you. Whether you have a developing or an established career, this book will truly help you get the position, recognition, and compensation you deserve by navigating your career negotiations.

INTRODUCTION

NEGOTIATE SMARTER AND AVOID MILLION-DOLLAR MISTAKES

*"You do not get what you want,
you get what you negotiate."*

Harvey Mackay

Most professionals lose 30 percent or more of the potential value of their compensation package with every position they take due to ineffective negotiations. *Millions* of dollars lost over the span of their careers, simply because they remain in the wrong positions too long or choose new positions poorly. These economic costs, however, pale in comparison to the loss of impactful business and social relationships, financial freedom, mental health, and strained family dynamics that often accompany those terrible decisions and compromises.

To make matters worse, these losses increase over time as employment missteps delay your professional development or prevent you from building the career you aspire to achieve within the time you have to achieve it. The consequences of these issues can permanently alter career course and trajectory, in some cases placing higher-end positions permanently out of reach.

Impossible to believe? Just think back to every position you have ever had and the actions you did or did not take that you now regret. Think about the opportunities for promotion that passed you by, the higher compensation you knew you could command but did not negotiate, the limited or lateral roles you settled on when you knew there could be better opportunities in the marketplace. The cumulative effect is extremely significant and arises from a lack of knowledge, experience, confidence, and training; ironically, the very opposite of the things you worked tirelessly to attain in your career.

These blind spots are devastating to promising careers. Thankfully, as we explore in this book, they are also easy to overcome. Once understood, you will immediately begin making better and well-informed decisions to reclaim the future career path you deserve. What we cover here is intuitive learning, which means you develop knowledge quickly and without any research or training to understand and you gain the ability to implement it immediately.

You have waited long enough. This book is for you if you have ever felt disenfranchised, overlooked, or sidelined. If you have ever kicked yourself because you did not ask – or felt you *could not* ask – for what you needed, wanted, or deserved, here is your opportunity for a huge comeback. Maybe you have made mistakes and want to course correct or reimagine your career and you need guidance to get it back on track. We will pull back the curtains on the corporate hiring machine, so you better understand and appreciate the true nature of employment dynamics through some of the most eye-opening misconceptions around employment negotiations. Debunking these tired old fallacies will cause necessary mindset shifts by leveling the playing field with employers, leading to truly impactful negotiations that include both tangible and intangible rewards. It is time to close the book on the knowledge gap.

CHAPTER ONE

ARE YOU BUYING OR SELLING WHEN IT COMES TO EMPLOYMENT OPPORTUNITIES?

"Too many people overvalue what they are not
and undervalue what they are."

Malcolm S. Forbes

You are the *seller*, not the buyer. If this feels backwards, you are not alone. This misconception has led professionals to make grievous errors in their negotiation strategies.

Your first reaction might be, "But there aren't buyers and sellers in relationships. That sounds like a business transaction!" You would be correct. The truth is that "employment relationship" is a highly inaccurate phrase.

All employment situations are, in reality, transactional.

Think about it. In what way do "employment relationships" seem like other relationships you have ever had? Answer: They do not. If you want to appreciate the absurdity of thinking of employment as a relationship, let us put it in social terms, like an employer might offer if you were dating:

> Our relationship is largely based on my terms unless we put something else in writing. You have to be monogamous and

dedicated to the relationship. I play the field. I can end our relationship without strings attached. In fact, I'll likely be dating someone else before I end our relationship without telling you or you knowing about it. You can end the relationship any time you want but I can restrict who you might want to date if I see them as competition. I get to tell you what to do during our relationship and will likely be critical of you in the process and expect you to change your behavior in ways that suit me. You don't have any of those privileges. How does that sound?

Lousy. Absolutely lousy. Does that sound like any relationship anyone would either find appealing or valuable? Of course not. Naturally, this is a ridiculous oversimplification. Many employment situations are fair and well balanced. But you get the point: the only way to truly appreciate employment relationships is to think about them the way they actually function – as a business transaction.

Every business transaction has a buyer and seller. From our earliest experiences, we learn to trade for value. In the elementary school lunchroom, Johnny will happily trade his PB&J for Zoe's chocolate pudding. A high school student will begrudgingly trade her summer vacation for that first job because she wants her first car more. We always bargain for the things we want or need. But somehow, we lose that bargaining perspective when it comes to employment relationships because we do not see each side as having something fundamental to offer the other. The problem is that only one side has learned how to consistently bargain effectively because they have mastered their part in the process. (Spoiler alert: It has historically *not* been the employee side.)

Since the evolution of the hiring concept, employers have been acutely aware that they are not selling anything. They are not "selling" you a position. *They are the buyers.* They are buying your time and talent. However, employees have always perceived that *they are the buyers*, agreeing to and accepting the terms and conditions of the job, just like signing a contract to purchase a car. This fundamental misunderstanding found its origins in the way employers present themselves during the job process and has cost employees millions of dollars and years of unnecessary setbacks.

When employers make a job offer, it is easy to believe that they are the sellers since they are presenting the deal and its terms. They are selling what you want, and you are negotiating to purchase it. This appears logical; thus, this mindset became part of the job process.

But this is completely wrong.

To be clear, employers are offering something, but they are not selling you *anything*. They have nothing to sell.

In fact, you are more than just the seller; you are literally the asset for sale! Your talents, expertise, network, influence, education, and experience are what you are selling. Those who have capitalized on their seller status and know their value have maximized their career trajectory and consequently had the most remarkable careers. Completing this shift in perspective is absolutely critical to success, and we will explore that later in this book.

But for now, know that you – the motivated career professional – are the value play. *You* are the asset with extraordinary value, and you, therefore, are the seller and the sale.

You Are the Asset

Professionals are the greatest capital asset employers will ever have: their most precious commodity. *Employees are the only asset capable of radical appreciation in value immediately upon acquisition and over time.* We challenge anyone to find an asset capable of being acquired by a business that can dynamically increase in value from the moment of purchase the way that an employee can. Not even the housing market can claim consistent appreciation. And that increased value translates into an *extraordinary* return on investment for the buyer/employer.

Every accomplishment, success, or advancement employees receive greatly benefits *their employer*. The employer who hires a vice president of marketing who later becomes chief marketing officer has acquired the asset (the VP turned CMO) without the need to go to the open market to hire someone at a cost much higher than the existing employee. The employer benefits because promoting that internal hire into a new role pales in comparison with the cost of hiring an experienced CMO from another organization. Promoting an existing employee who has already demonstrated his or her value and fit also benefits the employer because it avoids the possibility of a corporate culture mismatch.

If You Are the Seller, What Are You Selling Anyway?

Why does our negotiating stance hinge on the understanding that the employee is the seller, not the buyer? Simply put, because the most favorable terms cannot be attained without that realization.

When it comes to buying versus selling, there are key differences. Buying is getting something of value in exchange for compensation. Give a car dealership their price and receive the keys to your new car. The seller gets money, the buyer gets the asset.

Selling is the exact opposite. Selling typically involves receiving compensation in exchange for giving something away. The Apple Store collects a thousand dollars and the buyer leaves with a new iPhone.

Employees think that this analogy does not fit employment relationships because they are not selling anything, but every employee is in fact selling their time, the most precious commodity in the world. Time is precious for a wide variety of reasons in an employment context. Knowledge and expertise are developed via time spent on prior endeavors and this is extremely valuable to future employers. In return, employers will pay handsomely for that value since they directly benefit (i.e., the employer did not have to spend their time, money, or resources for someone to attain that skill set).

Employers understand the purpose of employment negotiations all too well and are looking to buy your time for the lowest cost. They are bargaining with you for the value of your time, but bargaining is *not* the problem. The problem is that you are willing to part with your time for much less than you should.

Having worked with thousands of clients in active job searches, Heather Dolan, SVP at Challenger, Gray & Christmas, is routinely told by clients working with her firm "I don't expect to get the same pay as I am getting right now."

Her response?

"Just because you are actively looking for a new role doesn't mean you are now on sale."

Heather says people who are actively pursuing employment seem to automatically assume their value dropped overnight (like driving a new car off the lot) and that they should compromise on their compensation before even leaving the starting gate. Put another way, we have all become *conditioned* to compromise.

Employees have historically believed they are required to settle for less, undervaluing their worth to obtain a position. You know that terrible internal voice that tells us to be grateful we are being offered anything at all. When you, as the potential employee, think of yourself as acquiring a position from an employer instead of selling your value, the employer has the upper hand in the bargaining process. When you realize that you are the seller, not the buyer, the mindset properly shifts into the correct position, and you can see employment situations for what they truly are: *the acquisition of your value by employers for a limited time.*

Sizing Up Negotiations Correctly Leads to an Amazing Revelation

Now that you know your bargaining position in the negotiation, you can better understand what you need to accomplish to be successful in the negotiation itself.

Every employment opportunity is of a temporary or indefinite nature, a stepping stone in your career journey. You are offered a position. That position lasts just as long as the employer or you want it to last and then the relationship ends. Shrewd employees develop their experience, then decide for themselves when the time is right to move on. That can be via a new employer, or they can assert themselves for promotion at their current place of employment and wait for the employer to offer more favorable roles or compensation terms to keep them employed.

Put simply, all you need to know about career building is this:

- *Sell* your time to an employer for the best compensation, professional growth, and least risk possible.
- *Build* new skill sets and experience while devoting your time on behalf of an employer.
- *Renegotiate* your terms of employment when the value of your time exceeds what you previously sold it for.
- *Seek* new employment when your current employer will not agree to renegotiate for mutually acceptable terms.

Understanding Your Leverage

Leverage is the ability of one side to influence the other in a negotiation to move closer to their position. A party's leverage is based on what it is trying to accomplish and what it has to offer. Put simply, if you do not understand which side of the negotiating table you are on, you have no leverage at the bargaining table.

If this seems a bit confusing, we completely understand. Heather often reminds me of the mental block about bargaining and leverage I had before I became a negotiation coach. But during a pivotal moment in my career, I finally understood why knowing one's bargaining position in an employment negotiation is so important.

I vividly remember applying for a senior associate position with a regional law firm, which would have been a lateral position for me. The firm asked me to meet with the head partner of the department to whom I would ultimately report as a formality, having already offered me the job. I felt like I was on autopilot, just going along with the process and making no attempt to negotiate the offer terms at all. Why had it not occurred to me to negotiate any aspect of the position, particularly given that I was overqualified for it?

Because it seemed like my dream job, and I did not want someone else to get it. See my flawed thinking there? Without realizing it, I had gone on the defense rather than the offense because I really wanted that position.

It was a lousy day all around, and I was anxious about losing the opportunity. During the interview, the head partner seemed extraordinarily condescending. I ignored his behavior – and my internal warnings – because I *really* wanted the job. The irony is that I was ready to accept whatever they handed me because I was so frustrated in my current position. But just as I was about to ignore all the glaring signs that this position was not right for me at all, the partner said, ". . . And look, if it doesn't work out, you can just go someplace else."

Wait a minute, I thought. *You are already positioning my value as minimal or subpar, and you know little or nothing about me?!* Instead of simply internalizing my frustration, however, my brain "lawyered up," and the assertive part of me, the part that I often harnessed for the benefit of clients, surfaced and took control.

What followed from my mouth sounded something like, "With all due respect, my career is not a salad bar for you to sample what you like and then just throw away."

To this day, I cannot remember my exact words, but I was a little embarrassed by how firmly I had asserted myself when I had so much on the line. I remember calling the legal recruiter after the interview and telling them I would never work there, no matter what they offered me. I realized it would be such an unpleasant place to spend my time, and I would be stuck with this partner at the top of the food chain.

The next day, the recruiter called and told me the COO of the firm wanted to personally meet me at my convenience to discuss what had transpired. Being more curious than anything else, I accepted his invitation. During that meeting, the COO told me that the partner I had interviewed with had reported back through the chain that no one had ever spoken to him in that manner, let alone an interviewee. Shockingly, he admired it because I had shown initiative he had not seen in years. So instead of offering me a senior associate position, the firm had a different offer in mind. *Partnership.*

I could not believe what I was hearing. I had no idea how such a ridiculous, impulsive comment on my part had fundamentally altered their impression of my value. With the benefit of hindsight, I do not believe it was the firm's impression of me in the interview process that sealed the deal. *It was the firm's recognition that I had truly appreciated my intrinsic value as a professional and had asserted myself.* My feeling that I had done something embarrassing was, in reality, a genuine expression of advocating for myself and so out of character that it caused me to second-guess my behavior. As human beings, we are so good at second-guessing ourselves that doubt and uncertainty become second nature, all to our detriment.

This assessment and prioritizing of your own value is the difference between one-sided negotiation, which gives employers the upper hand, and a mutually beneficial negotiation. This assertiveness is happening with greater frequency and impact these days. If you have experienced that awakening recently, you are not alone.

In 2021, Texas A&M University professor Anthony Klotz coined the term "the Great Resignation"[1] to encapsulate the seismic shift of the workforce post-pandemic. Professor Klotz was undoubtedly paying homage to the Great Depression of 1929, a result of the stock market crash that year. Similarly, the Great Resignation is a reaction or result of post-pandemic thinking. While COVID-19's impact on the workforce is well known, the multiple reasons behind it are less understood. Of the reasons posited in *The Boston Globe* article, one stands out more than the rest: "Lots of people were having revelations about how they wanted to spend their time moving forward."

But the reaction to the pandemic is not properly framed as a resignation. That is a result or by-product – a reaction to something. A more apt analogy would be the reevaluation or assessment of self-worth in a job market. The pandemic gave professionals a unique opportunity for a contemplative pause necessary to reevaluate their worth and how they spend their time. A new appreciation of mortality tends to have that effect on people.

Self-realization. Self-awareness. Self-validation. Knowing your value is priceless and so empowering that it can lead you to consider your trajectory. Are you where you want to be, and where are you heading? Fortune favors the bold. This is the essence of career advancement.

---

1   Anissa Gardizy, "'The Great Resignation' is looming: Why people are quitting their jobs post-pandemic," The Boston Globe, June 22, 2021, https://www.bostonglobe.com/2021/06/22/business/burnout-is-one-key-predictors-turnover-what-know-about-great-resignation/.

> Professionals are the sellers of highly prized valuable services. Know your worth!

CHAPTER TWO

WHAT ARE YOU REALLY NEGOTIATING FOR (BEYOND THE MONEY)?

*"If everyone is thinking alike,
then somebody isn't thinking."*

George S. Patton

So, now we know who we are and what our side of the table looks like in the negotiation process. But what is each side trying to accomplish in that process? The answer is not merely an agreement on favorable terms. Employers and employees are not negotiating for the same thing from different sides of the table. They each have an agenda that is the exact opposite of what the other side wants out of the relationship, and understanding these core concepts gives us great insight into how employers approach employment negotiations.

Most professionals believe that employers want things like maximum control, perfect performance, and the cheapest salary and benefits possible, while employees want to make the most money with the most independence. Sure, those may be aspects or elements of what employers would like to get out of the relationship, but that is not what they are bargaining for in the negotiation process. You may think it is control, and you would be close, but it is about something a bit more subtle.

It is their ability to purchase your time free of any limitation, without any accountability to you, and regardless of any negative impact to your career.

Indefinite Plans

Every aspect of employment offered by an employer has *flexibility* at its core, because every term drafted by an employer is framed around the concept of **at-will employment**. But most professionals do not understand how broad that concept really is or what it truly represents, because it is not just about deciding to hire or end the relationship. According to the National Conference of State Legislatures, at-will employment is defined as the following:[2]

> At-will means that an employer can terminate an employee at any time for any reason, except an illegal one, or for no reason without incurring legal liability. Likewise, an employee is free to leave a job at any time for any or no reason with no adverse legal consequences.
>
> *At-will also means that an employer can change the terms of the employment relationship with no notice and no consequences* [emphasis added].

For example, an employer can alter wages, terminate benefits, or reduce paid time off. In its unadulterated form, the U.S. at-will rule leaves employees vulnerable to arbitrary and sudden dismissal, a limited or on-call work schedule depending on the employer's needs, and unannounced cuts in pay and benefits.

---

2   "At-Will Employment—Overview," National Conference of State Legis-latures, April 15, 2008, https://www.ncsl.org/research/labor-and-employment/at-will-employment-overview.aspx.

Put another way, at-will employment is a far-reaching concept. Not just to make decisions at the beginning and end of an employment relationship but to change everything in between when it suits the employer's purpose to do so.

Employers are looking for ultimate flexibility in a relationship largely on their terms. They thoughtfully court you with interviews, present you with a verbal offer, and then add in all that legal jargon, limited terms, and caveats to the written offer. What employers want when they get to the written stage is to have you agree to give them the power over every aspect of the relationship. This includes when they pay you, how much they pay you, and whether and when you get your bonus while limiting any discussion of your rights, responsibilities and so forth.

But the ultimate expression of this at-will concept is the employer's interest in having flexibility that extends beyond the employment relationship. We have seen far too many cases of restrictions on an employee's post-employment opportunities via non-compete agreements that could preclude you from working in entire industries, even if they lay you off without notice and without cause. Without suitable protections, these limitations can literally keep you from making a living in your chosen field or industry. Employers want the ability to deploy or eliminate assets in the manner they wish, when they wish, and with as little accountability as possible. They want all the risk of the relationship to rest squarely on your shoulders, not theirs. You might as well call this "employment at whim"!

Certain Futures

Professionals do not want nebulous constructs like indefinite employment relationships; they want definition, clearly detailed expectations, and aligned expectations. They want a fifty-page employment offer that delineates every aspect of the agreement, including the method of payment and frequency, specific responsibilities, guaranteed promotions and bonuses, and so on. Professionals also want clear-cut, limited, or narrow parameters on when and how they can be terminated. Ultimately, the employee wants an agreement the size of a textbook, and the employer wants a half-page agreement.

Realistically, neither side ever gets their wish.

So, given these disparate agendas, how do we handle employment negotiations to navigate away from the professional carrying all the risk and having none of the desired specificity necessary to ensure their success?

Leverage your skills to convince your prospective employer to define success for your role in the employment offer letter or agreement. The trick is to get to "yes" without turning the negotiation adversarial and poisoning an otherwise promising relationship before it starts. This win/win strategy is called "Non-Zero Sum", as shown below.

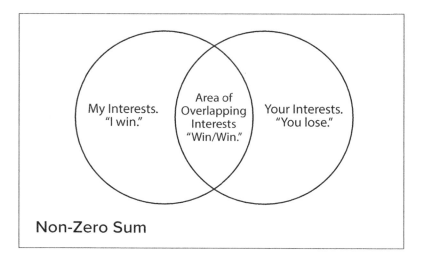

So how do professionals manage the dynamic of the employment negotiation while maintaining the correct attitude to ensure success? By recognizing or appreciating the inherent limitations on employers and the rules of play. The employer must be allowed to maintain some autonomy to manage the relationship while giving the employee a definitive understanding of their role, responsibilities, and rules of engagement.

Clearly, the employer lacks a crystal ball to make salary determinations five years from now, but they should agree to a salary review each year if asked. They cannot guarantee a promotion every year but should be able to tell you in general terms when you would be eligible for one. You cannot tell an employer that they cannot fire you without your consent, but you can reach a proactive agreement to mitigate against the financial burden of an unexpected job loss through **severance** and substantial **notice periods** (more on that later).

Savvy professionals know that all employment negotiations have a give and take. Employers need to lead the dance with the framing and presentation of an offer, and you need to demonstrate your value as a potential hire and why you will be a great dance partner. Your leverage will make the employer more willing to compromise some flexibility in order to give you some of the certainty you need.

Employment relationships balance flexibility and certainty, just like the agreements reflecting them.

CHAPTER THREE

DO YOU ACTUALLY KNOW WHO YOU ARE GOING TO WORK FOR?

"When a person shows you who they are, believe them."

Maya Angelou

Paying close attention to how your current or prospective employer behaves at the bargaining table is also a critical aspect of employment negotiations. In the euphoria that follows the completion of a successful negotiation, many professionals forget that their treatment in the negotiation process is often a preview of what it will be like to work for their employer. Troubling personality traits or mannerisms shown by the employer during negotiations are very likely to be repeated when you start working for that employer. This is why it is critical to consider your treatment in the process when deciding whether or not to accept an offer.

Remember, the time before you start your employment is the honeymoon stage in your employment relationship. If the employer demonstrates flexibility in negotiation and willingness to compromise, you will likely find that same fluidity in their managerial approach. Being receptive to questions and open to topics like expectations, workplace culture, and managerial style are all good signs of a positive work relationship. Conversely, inflexibility without explanation, conversations that feel forced or stilted (particularly with your new boss), and emotional reactions like exasperation or frustration on the part of your employer all give strong indications of what you might be in for when you start the job. Do not ignore the warning signs.

Trust but Verify

Malcolm Gladwell talks about the concept of trust at face value in his book *Talking to Strangers*. For inexplicable reasons, this phenomenon is part of human nature. We often overestimate our ability to judge strangers, and thus, we tend to accept blindly what other people – even strangers – tell us without question. One particularly salient example Gladwell explores concerned a majority of senior British politicians and military strategists who believed, based on a few meetings with Adolf Hitler, that he had no ambitions to expand his empire beyond old Germanic borders. They simply took Hitler at his word. Why? Because they expected him to act in a certain way based on the limited information they had and their views of social norms displayed by other leaders of that era. With the stakes being so high, their overconfidence was catastrophic.

This behavioral "acceptance" happens to each of us in our personal lives every day. When we meet someone at a networking function and that person tells us that they are the chief financial officer of a business, we likely believe them. But why? What has this person done to earn our trust in the reliability of anything they say? Nothing! So why take the information at face value? We do this partly because we assume based on our expectations of human behavior that this person has nothing to gain from lying to us. *But more importantly, we have no significant interest in confirming the truth.* Whether this person is telling the truth has no major impact on us because we are not acting on the information. We go through life like this with most of the people we meet. We assume they are who they say they are, and we relate to them based on what they tell us about themselves. This probably explains why so many of us fall prey to fake news, internet scams, and other false presentations of information. We just trust certain things to be how they appear.

You *cannot* afford to do this in a hiring context. The employment world is a venue where blind acceptance of facts (or worse, being told you need to "trust" your employer) can be catastrophically damaging to your career. You may only have a handful of discussions about your role before needing to make a decision. Accepting a job based solely on what you are told without the ability to confirm the information can have devastating and permanent consequences.

You cannot assume that everything you are told is completely accurate when the stakes are so high. In a 1987 op-ed, *The New York Times* brought back an old Russian proverb: "Trust but verify." This is the best way to judge information.

So how do you trust but verify? To do so, you need as much independent data as you can possibly obtain. You would never buy a used car without a full inspection, even if you had a report on the car's condition and a family member was selling it to you, because you just do not know the actual condition of the car. Even the most well-intentioned person may not know that the car has problems or is in the process of developing them. So why would you ever take something as important or critical as a job offer at face value without a deep dive into the details? In the corporate world, we refer to this process as "due diligence," the way in which every purchase and sale of a business is handled. It refers to the appraisal of a business by a buyer to assess its assets and liabilities to evaluate its potential.

You need to think like you would *if you were buying the business itself* rather than being employed by the business when sizing up a new employment opportunity. We have included a comprehensive summary checklist to use when gathering information in your own due diligence process in the Appendix to this book, but all the relevant questions need to be answered. If satisfactory answers are not immediately provided, dig deeper or go up the chain. Chase down all the "I'll get back to you" and "Let's follow up on that" communications you receive. Do not be intimidated. It is infinitely better to get these answers up front to make an informed decision than to realize a mistake after signing on the proverbial dotted line.

It is not just the employer's answers themselves that are important data points. The employer's reaction to your inquiries is as important as the answers themselves. If they seem to balk at or waffle on the answers, appear uncertain about the subject matter, or try to push off the conversation, this should be a red flag and you need to pursue your inquiries further or with more senior employees before you proceed to accept employment under the terms of the offer.

Read the Signs

Employers often telegraph what it will actually be like to work with them through five clear signals:

1. Communication style
2. Body language
3. Demeanor
4. Approach
5. Responsiveness (in terms of timing and detail)

Each facet of the negotiation process is revealing, and most employers will show their true colors as the negotiations unfold. Watch how the company handles the interview process itself. Note those in attendance during the interviews and again later when the offer is presented (typically a verbal offer followed by a written one). Pay particular attention to whether you are encouraged or permitted to meet with your direct reports prior to accepting the position. Observe the extent of involvement of senior leadership if you are taking a C-suite or similar position. Assess to the depth or detail of their responses, particularly with respect to the future growth and development of the organization and the part you will play (and the recognition you will receive) in accomplishing that growth and development.

If the interview team represents personnel from various groups or divisions of the company, you know the company is looking for cross-checks to support your hiring. That is a good sign of the prospective employer's view of the significance of hiring you. Similarly, pay particular attention to the promotion trajectory; if there is no clearly defined career path available beyond the intended position, it is unlikely that the company has an advancement path to keep your career progression on target with your goals. If it looks like a siloed position without a future path, it is more likely that the company simply needs someone to fill the position in the short term, not that it needs *you* to fill the position for a long-term role. "Body in the seat" roles are terrible for career development and will never lend themselves to a positive career trajectory for you.

Then there is the issue of the reporting structure, which is depicted on organizational charts as the **reporting line**. The reporting line defines your relationship to those you work for and who work for you. Developing some perspective about your manager is an extremely important part of the interview process. What have you gleaned about working for that person from your interactions thus far? The manager's LinkedIn profile might also give you some interesting insight or perspective about them, and your own network might know something you do not know about working for them. What do you know about them based on their mannerisms, idiosyncrasies, and body language? Have you perceived or witnessed any interactions that suggest a lack of respect, inflammatory language, or worse, a suggestion of negative treatment of other direct reports or teammates? Maligning someone's own team is a dead giveaway of a toxic or negative work environment, particularly if you are replacing someone in that team as a direct report. Nothing can derail a career faster than reporting to someone who is toxic.

Assess the Sticking Points

Sticking points are the terms you need but are having a hard time getting the employer to accept. What rationale does the employer provide when they push back on requests or asks? If the reaction is simply, "We don't do things that way here," that could be revealing a rigidity that will undermine your goals and aspirations as an employee. Sometimes the sticking points actually relate to your position level, which is perfectly reasonable for the employer to use as a reason to reject a request. If you are too junior to make those requests (e.g., severance protection for a job loss that is not offered to director-level candidates), then you know that your asks rather than the employer's mindset are the problem, and the prospective employer may very well make better offers to more senior prospective hires.

Know When to Walk Away, Know When to Run

An employer who will not bargain directly with you when asked and insists on using intermediaries like headhunters or recruiters suggests an indifference to you that foreshadows a terrible employment relationship. When your potential supervisor or their boss will not give you the time of day over things that concern you in a prospective relationship, you need to run. Be wary of accepting a position based on difficult, unilateral negotiations. You may find management just as difficult to deal with on a daily basis.

Similarly, if a prospective employer is not being transparent in negotiations with you, expect the same treatment once you become an employee. A lack of transparency can include the omission of key details discovered during your own due diligence research, such as potential mergers, bankruptcies, downsizing, lawsuits, or takeovers. They might also misrepresent whether they have different versions of contracts depending on your level (e.g., C-suites may have better terms and conditions they are willing to offer).

Gut Reactions Really Matter: Four Paradigms

There has been an almost perfect 1:1 correlation between the instinctive reactions professionals have had about their prospective employers and the resulting experiences. When professionals have accepted offers based on engaged employers (i.e., employers willing to put the time in to address their reasonable asks), working for those employers has typically been a positive experience for them. Alternatively, clients who have accepted jobs with employers who rubbed them the wrong way in the negotiations process have found that dynamic continued and wish they had passed on the opportunity.

Be wary of the following archetypes while progressing through the hiring process.

Passive-Aggressive Employers

A candidate is offered a position as a senior director following rocky interviews with a passive-aggressive CEO. The CEO requests the candidate's feedback on the offer and even suggests hiring an attorney to review the offer. After review, the candidate makes modest changes, including a title change and minor modifications to the contract to protect his earned bonus. The CEO becomes aggressive and hypercritical about the changes and rejects them without even a conversation. He even articulates his disappointment with his requests. The candidate then passes on the opportunity realizing that this behavior would likely escalate once he started working there. Knee jerk reactions like those exhibited by this CEO are warning signs for anyone thinking about working for someone like that. If you spot behavior like this during the negotiation process you can expect things will be ten times worse once the employment relationship begins.

Employers Insisting on Trust before an Agreement Is Signed

A candidate applies for a senior vice president (SVP) role but has concerns about the opportunity. The company will not agree to integrate her **position description**, bonus criteria, or a **Good Reason** clause into the agreement. The CEO responds with outrage, stating that by insisting on having these terms incorporated into the agreement, she was implying she had a lack of trust in the company to honor its verbal promises and commitments. He chastises her by saying that she must trust that the company will do the right thing. Under duress, the candidate relents. Regrettably, she learns that all her concerns were legitimate. She receives a subpar bonus, her position changes radically from what she expected, and she is ultimately forced to leave the job to avoid further mistreatment without any severance. Proceed with extreme caution when the employer demands trust up front to negate the need for reasonable written assurances. No candidate has any requirement to trust a prospective employer at the outset of an employment relationship. Trust must always be earned and takes time to occur.

Employers Who Reject Requests That Do Not Cost the Company Anything

Another candidate in an existing SVP role is contemplating a switch to a new company that offers more than just a lateral move as he ultimately seeks the role of chief financial officer (CFO). However, the candidate is not thought to be experienced enough to obtain that position. The candidate is understandably fearful of a lateral move because it will make his career look as though it is stagnating. The SVP, fortunately, obtains offers of employment from two different companies. On paper, one seems more lucrative, but management has an inflexible approach to discussions about the future path to CFO. The offer from the second company is less attractive financially, but the company is more open to a discussion about promotion to CFO.

The candidate tests the resolve of both companies, asking whether they would be willing to put in writing the period of time that the SVP has to wait before being eligible for consideration for promotion to C-suite. (Remember, all that the candidate asked was to be considered, not to be promoted.) The first company rejects the request. The second company is willing to put in writing that the candidate would be considered for promotion a year after his start. The candidate took the second position, and the company promoted him to the C-suite role in the following year. Beware of shortsighted or myopic employers like the first company, who were well aware of the fact that it cost them nothing to offer what the candidate asked for and passed on it anyway. If this is how your employer behaves when you ask for so little, imagine what will happen when you have important asks, like salary increases or promotional opportunities!

Employers Who Cannot Be Taken at Their Word

A candidate negotiates an offer for a Mergers and Acquisitions position. The company provides detailed spreadsheets illustrating the metrics of how bonuses are calculated. The bonus structure in the offer letter is reliant on that strategy, and the company insists that the bonus documents are complete as presented. The candidate accepts the structure and, ultimately, the employment offer. The company also tells the candidate that they will be sending an employment agreement that would replace the offer letter but would contain the same terms. The candidate learns to his unfortunate dismay that the employment agreement radically deviated from the offer letter. Among other things, the employment agreement contained a completely new and less advantageous bonus structure with no reference to the old metrics as well as draconian non-compete restrictions. The company neither explained, acknowledged, nor apologized for the fact that the two documents were so different. Of course, the professional was forced to hire an attorney at his own expense and renegotiate a new series of terms and conditions only to ultimately pass on the opportunity – a true waste of time and effort for everyone.

Only *one* of the employers in these examples recognizes that it costs them nothing to make requested changes to an employment relationship, and doing so engenders trust and confidence on both sides. Unfortunately, employers are making these myopic mistakes with great frequency; thus, employees are too often left to bear the full weight of the consequences after proceeding, despite these red flags.

Never negotiate your self-worth
or sell yourself short for the sake of a job.

CHAPTER FOUR

WHY IS FOCUSING ON SALARY THE WORST WAY TO NEGOTIATE TERMS OF EMPLOYMENT?

> ""If you undervalue what you do, the world undervalues who you are. And when you undervalue who you are, the world undervalues what you do."
>
> *Suze Orman*

Throughout history, the word "value" has been synonymous with "money," but this is overly simplistic. When employment negotiations predominantly focus on the cash associated with an opportunity, major problems occur. Compensation, in fact, is the LAST thing to negotiate in the hiring process.

We recognize this feels counterintuitive to most people. Payment becomes the principal focus of an employment contract or offer because it is the most tangible component of the relationship.

Compensation is also the easiest part of an employment offer to grasp because it is instantaneously relatable. Your paycheck, in part, defines your contribution and how your employer perceives your value. However, we want to break the mindset that the word "compensation" is interchangeable with "salary" because a salary is a part of a much larger compensation package that, in many cases, is much more lucrative than the salary component itself and is frequently overlooked. Compensation can be structured in three different ways: **fixed compensation**, **variable compensation**, and **benefits**. While fixed compensation is typically immediate, like base salary, variable compensation is performance based and includes rewards like commission, stock options, bonus pools, and phantom or synthetic equity (a payout only on sale or company exit).

Variable compensation and benefits often have greater value than fixed compensation, particularly when you have a sizable target bonus representing 30 percent or more of your base salary and health care benefits that can offset substantial medical bills.

This discussion highlights why compensation is such an important driver of employment negotiations that the size of its perceived impact overshadows everything else. The anxious among us cannot wait for the verbal offer from their potential new employer. Of course, this is the trap. Sure, you need to know that the offer aligns with your needs and expectations. But consider this: Compensation is the *outcome* of the employer's evaluation of your total value assessment after everything else is negotiated properly. By leading with this discussion prematurely, you are underselling yourself because the employer has not appropriately grasped *all the value you bring* to the company – *you will leave money on the table!*

Imagine you are trying to sell a car. If you really wanted to get top dollar for it, you would describe the most critical selling features of the car (performance, efficiency, mileage, storage space, rows of seats) before presenting the price. If you do not make a concerted effort to highlight the benefits of what you are offering, you are grossly undercutting your own interests. In fact, when you undersell yourself, you give an employer pause about hiring you in the first place and may never get to a discussion of compensation.

There is another critical reason that compensation needs to be put into perspective. It is just numbers on paper. There is nothing real about compensation terms written in your employment offer. Yes, we realize that this, too, sounds counterintuitive. We know that you might currently be holding a job offer letter clearly delineating how much salary they are offering. How can we be so flippant? Well, you probably believe that when you start the job, that is what you will get. Actually, that is not correct at all because there is generally only one thing in any offer letter or agreement that you can count on. (Spoiler alert: It has nothing to do with compensation.)

A start date. That is it. That is the only dependable part of an employment offer.

No matter what you think you are getting out of an offer letter, the employer is only offering you the *potential* to capture the financial terms and conditions set forth in the employment offer or agreement. You must stay long enough in the employment relationship to get those terms.

We realize it is very hard for most people to accept this premise. After all, when we look at the offer letter, it seems to clearly delineate all those important tangible components, right? But employment relationships just are not structured that way. Everything is contingent. That offer letter offers no guarantees about anything.

So, if the money is a contingent part of an employment offer, at least it is something tangible and real for as long as it lasts.

"What could possibly be more important to get right than money?" you ask.

The thing that makes or breaks the duration of the deal – your role or position in the company.

The Crown Jewel of All Employment Offers Is an *Intangible*: Role

We have already discussed why the "employee is the buyer" model is incorrect and results in lost opportunities for the employee. We also understand that our biggest asset as sellers/employees is our time. However, the most difficult part of the negotiation is to understand that to *maximize your career trajectory*, you need to properly negotiate one intangible item. Successfully getting this item right will aid in achieving the hallmarks of a successful career, including the best pay, authority, recognition, and marketability available to you. The most important thing to negotiate is your *role*.

A role defines the particular job function or activity of our work for an employer. Role has nothing to do with who we are as individuals or our character, beliefs, experiences, or values. We personalize roles by pouring those personal elements into them, and that shapes how we serve in the roles.

The primary element for negotiation is defining your role properly. This includes not just your duties and responsibilities but also your actual title. Any upward deviation or modification from an offered role can lead to extraordinary increases in value. Position is the most important part of a negotiation, and yet, ironically, *positions have no fixed, intrinsic, or intangible value whatsoever*. Role frames the entire nature of the position you are bargaining for, including your function, duties and responsibilities, **span of authority and control**, reporting line, and its significance both internally and externally to the organization. The role is the entirety of the meaning of an employment opportunity and what you are really bargaining to obtain from an employer. Even if the job is ultimately a poor fit, that role can go on your resume. It is now part of your career journey. For these reasons, obtaining the right position is critical. You would never want to accept a position or a title that sounds like a step down, even if it is accompanied by a raise.

More importantly, your new title will set the stage for your *next* position, too. If it appears to be a step down, the next person to look at your resume will assume it was, and you may or may not have an opportunity to refute that. When you accept a role and a job offer, you are hopefully setting yourself up for success in the current position as well as laying the groundwork for successful negotiation in your next role. **Job titles** matter as much as the position description. Should you have any input into its description, framing your job title is an important element of your negotiations. Internally, your job title determines how others view your responsibility and rank within your organization (director, officer, etc.). Externally, a title defines your level of experience.

Never accept a title that seems made up or is out of sync with your industry. For example, Global Head of XYZ may mean a great deal in the tech industry but means little in pharma. If your title would not be instantly understood to reflect an appropriate level both within and outside of the employer by a talent recruiter, a client, or a customer, it needs an adjustment.

Employers Will Negotiate Almost Anything

Let us get one thing out of the way first. Many employees believe that when an offer is presented, employers will not negotiate terms other than compensation. Remember that concept of flexibility? It extends to everything an employer does. So, by extension, employers will negotiate virtually anything. Your negotiating power entirely depends upon your leverage, your experience, your age, what they need, the supply of applicants, the demand for employees, the scope of the job, and to what extent you are bargaining within reasonable compensation ranges based on market conditions.

You can even negotiate your reporting line to lock who you will report to during employment, something that can be absolutely essential to success in a new role. For instance, let us say you are a marketing director who reports to the chief marketing officer. Guess what? Tomorrow they could hire a senior director of marketing, a VP of marketing and an SVP of marketing. Suddenly, instead of reporting into the C-suite, there are now four layers between you and the C-suite. Naturally, your employer never telegraphed that they intended to make those moves. What is worse is that you never asked.

You may like a position because the prospective employer currently has a flat reporting structure (i.e., there are not many intervening layers between your position and the C-suites or top management level). But there is no guarantee that an organization is going to remain flat! Any commitment by an employer that you will continue to report into the C-suite level would have to be written into your agreement. Without that stipulation, the employer can put as many layers between you and the management team as they please. This would ultimately make your position at the employer appear more junior than it did when you were initially hired and also deprive you of the experience and attention of the top-level employees of the company.

Most senior executives still do not realize that they can negotiate these aspects of an employment relationship. This is not surprising given that it usually takes experience in more advanced roles to appreciate your leverage to make these requests. Many professionals lack an experienced confidante to help educate them as to what others have successfully negotiated or what pitfalls to avoid. Thus, they turn to less professionally reliable sources, including friends and family, who while well intentioned may not understand the nuances of their professional journey like a mentor or coach would. This problem is more acutely felt by women and minorities who in many cases are coming into senior-level roles for the first time without counterparts, mentors, or sponsors.

Why We Often Negotiate Roles Poorly

Although getting roles set at the right level and defined properly is the primary goal of every successful employment negotiation, the negotiation process itself can feel daunting or even overwhelming. We get so caught up in what we believe to be the value of the employment opportunity itself that we forget it is just one potential role, and there are many others out there in the marketplace.

Like so many other things about the employment world, we put so much pressure on ourselves to get the jobs we want, fearing what our futures look like without them, that we find it hard to look at them constructively. These three linked concepts are part of our decision-making process and influence our thinking about roles:

- Who we are (our personal identity).
- What we actually do for a living (our work).
- Why we want a particular career (our purpose).

Add ego (self-esteem or self-importance) into the mix and you have a recipe for making all kinds of bad employment decisions in selecting roles.

Our ego deceives us into believing we derive or develop true meaning or value in our lives from the roles we serve. Ego leads us there because we want to see our employment experiences as valuable, given the time we devote to them, and thereby create or construct a belief that our positions give us our purpose or identity.

In truth, it is the exact opposite.

While roles may shape our thinking about ourselves, our views as to who we are and what we want out of our careers existed long before we became employees and will exist long after we leave our employment roles behind.

We have all heard in our lives some variant of the phrase, "What you do is not who you are," and it has become such a cliché that we recite it as a mantra without really understanding what it means. Emily Rudow has a great take on the subject in general terms in *The New York Times*.[2] But let us get more specific about role as it pertains to employment negotiations.

In other words, we channel our identity and our purpose into our work.

Understandably, many of us do not think of roles in such simple terms. We think of our roles as if they are the most critical part of our identity, that we derive purpose in our lives from the roles we play. While we all hate to admit it, most of us fall into that trap. We validate ourselves by our careers rather than by who we are or what drives our need to succeed in our careers.

---

2   Emily Rudow, "Who You Are is Not What You Do," Emily Rudow, January 13, 2022, https://emilyrudow.com/blog/who-you-are-is-not-what-you-do/.

Validating ourselves through our employment relationships has a devastating impact on our ability to negotiate effectively. That mindset of craving validation often leads to perceiving a prospective employer more positively than is deserved or than circumstances would suggest. The result is that professionals can leave their current position for the wrong reasons based on a promise of an improved position and repeat the cycle by joining a new employer who makes grandiose promises.

For example, a VP of sales is considering an SVP role for less money at a smaller company with big promises of future advancement. The VP's unhappiness in his current job leads to the following thought: *Well, the salary is not as good as it should be, but I need the advancement and recognition I am not getting in my current position, and I deserve that better title.* The desire for recognition may cloud the judgment of this VP in taking the new position when the position may not benefit the VP in the long term, because a title itself is only one indicator of a successful career move.

This is just one example of how difficult it sometimes is to distinguish our personal identity or purpose from our position. We forget that personal identity evolves over time and that purpose is a lifetime achievement. Instead, the tendency is to dwell on a current job or prospective offer as if that is the essence of our personality. For instance, role compensation helps define a person's value, and role significance helps define a person's status. The danger, however, is that you define yourself by a role or position to the exclusion of every other worthwhile aspect of your life. When you have no personal identity outside of the immediacy of your role, self-worth is solely determined by job successes and failures, which is never a healthy situation.

So how do we properly understand these three concepts and how they operate in an employment context? Work is what we choose to do for a living. Identity defines how we perform our work. Purpose is the *why* of what we do. Viewed in this way, a role is the function we serve at work or what we do along the way to fulfilling our personal identity or serving our purpose. Aligning our identity and purpose with the roles we select for ourselves is what gives us the best opportunity to maximize our career potential and trajectory. The opposite is also true.

A great example of understanding the interplay between a professional's work, identity, and purpose and how to align them in selecting a given role comes from these two famous actors: Hugh Jackman and Christopher Reeve. What both actors had in common is that they decided to gamble on themselves by making a risky jump to the silver screen. That was part of advancing the purpose of their careers. Both individuals were already accomplished actors with brilliant theater careers who chose completely unfamiliar roles (as superheroes!) to serve as the springboard to major film careers. They brought their unique perspectives to these roles based on experience (i.e., their identities), and their move to these roles was a calculated risk that their performances would lead to other rewarding opportunities. However, when they left the set, they no longer saw themselves in these actor roles. They could separate the roles they played from their own personas.

We need to think about roles the same way, by putting them in perspective the way actors do. Recognize their importance but not make them our whole identity. Perform our roles according to our values and beliefs and how the roles contribute to fulfilling the purposes of our careers but not confuse them with who we are in a personal sense. Because setting our roles correctly can lead to greater success in our careers, including greatly improved compensation. Conversely, defining ourselves by our roles can actually hurt our ability to objectively assess the roles we want and reduce the value of the positions we deserve by accepting them.

Sophia Davis is a recruiter and the founder of Bio Directors, LLC, and BioPharm Physicians, LLC. For over twenty-five years, her experience has been in the biopharmaceutical industry, recruiting physician executives and directors for major biopharma companies around the world. Sophia has a sound take on the importance of role selection: "If the new opportunity doesn't bring you closer to your goal (relevant new skills, upward mobility, etc.) all it will do is delay you from getting there."

In other words, if you do not understand how every role you take on furthers your advancement, fulfills your purpose, and serves your personal identity, there is no way to guarantee that your career will benefit from accepting any of them.

The right mindset on role can have an amazing impact on the other aspects of your position, particularly compensation. Here are a few examples of how advanced thinking about roles leads to greater value in your negotiations.

Three Case Studies of Role Impact on Compensation

Executive A negotiates for a VP role at $200,000. She advises the employer that a VP role of this nature would be a lateral role that would not benefit her interest in career advancement. She successfully negotiates a role as SVP of clinical operations. Instantaneously, she reaps an enormous increase from the value of the new title.

The employer increases the offer to $300,000 before she even has to make a counter and adds a range of benefits and other considerations that were not previously offered.

Executive B negotiates for the same VP role at $200,000. She advises the employer that she requires additional compensation for the role based on various industry markers, experience, etc., unknowingly limiting her growth and missing a greater opportunity. The parties settle on $225,000, because the company is unwilling to increase the salary offer based on the **salary band** limitations of the VP position. Negotiating for salary before negotiating for the role ultimately damages her negotiations, her role, and her compensation.

Executive C takes a step forward in position but *backward* in pay from a senior director role (from $275,000) at a large established pharmaceutical company where there is no opportunity for advancement to a VP role at a startup pharmaceutical company with a promising new drug in clinical trials (new salary: $225,000). Additionally, she is offered a generous equity package. All things being equal, that advancement in position has enormous value in her career and demonstrates initiative at the same time. The risk of failure is properly assessed, because if the job does not pan out, the newly minted officer can leverage her new title to find another position down the road with a greater compensation package than she had at the large pharma company.

These examples provide insight as to why negotiating for salary alone is potentially pennywise, pound foolish, and results in a career trajectory that loses both compensation and momentum.

Opportunity Costs: The Most Overlooked Variable

Opportunity cost is another important variable that career professionals must consider before negotiating compensation.

This term addresses the impact associated with a move from one position or company to another, which has real-world consequences. For example:

- Moving from a position with no non-compete to one with an overbearing non-compete.
- Forfeiting vested equity due to early departure in order to join a company that does not offer equity.
- Being required to change from remote work back to a physical office.
- Being forced to repay a sign-on bonus or moving stipend because you voluntarily quit.

Only when you look at role and opportunity cost can you tackle compensation, particularly since you need to weigh the value of the role against the opportunity cost (or risks) of accepting it. Believing that securing great compensation will offset a flawed role choice or massive opportunity costs could be one of the costliest mistakes of your career.

If the role does not align properly with your desired career trajectory or if the opportunity costs are excessive, you will not last long enough in the role to break even on your compensation. As a result, you may very well trade away your ability to find a great new employment opportunity. Be prepared to walk away if the role is an improper fit, regardless of a seemingly attractive compensation. Or be ready to negotiate harder.

Now We Can Talk About Compensation

Employers have salary bands for most roles. When you are analyzing an employment offer, it behooves both sides to get these data points. But there is something more fundamental to understand first: your own value. Knowing what someone is willing to pay for your time is irrelevant if you do not have a benchmark to measure it against. This is where industry standards, peer review, and experience play a critical role. There are also a number of third-party sites that actually provide salary information on an industry basis, depending upon the role that you are looking for, and your colleagues probably know this information too. In this case, Google is your friend.

The worst thing you can do is to assume that your current salary is the best gauge for salary discussions. While your current salary offer is a starting point for comparison as a baseline value, it is a misleading data point. There is no standardized rate for anything. There is a range of values depending on region, industry, position, experience, and sector, to name a few. Labor demand and supply are also critical factors. Each of these variables plays a key role in the final number. But remember that the employer has salary limits as well. They will be constrained by salary bands, budgets, internal assessments, and many more factors. So, the topic will come up no matter how neatly or nicely you dodge the question or deflect it.

When the employer asks the inevitable question about your salary requirements, focus on the salary range and discuss employer expectations of you in the position. Use *only* the upper range in your discussions and justify your position as to why that upper number is the relevant number for you. This is your time to start a discussion connecting your value with a financial range. Your value is a way to explain why you are entitled to receive the upper number of that range. If the position is not available in your desired salary range, assess how far off it is and what tradeoffs you can accept to meet your needs. Remember that there is compensation data available from various sources to help gauge what you can and should earn in the marketplace. You can also approach recruiters and compensation coaches to help you with an appraisal of your value. Do not go it alone! More on that later.

Watch Your Step: The Pitfalls in Employment Agreements

Even when you have negotiated the three dimensions of an employment relationship properly (role, opportunity cost, and compensation), be wary. The next step is the employment agreement itself. The employer is likely to be a seasoned negotiator, and they are not going to be forthcoming with all of the information you might want to have before signing that offer letter. In fact, they may deliberately limit what they want you to know. There are also various loopholes and perils contained in every written employment agreement, and the relationship between employer and employee is still one of strangers vying for a bargain on terms more favorable to one side than the other. Accordingly, the employer is not going to sit down with you and go line by line explaining terms and conditions that may be unfamiliar to you. Proceeding without the right guidance can be a disaster for the professional who simply assumes the terms in the employment offer are fair and balanced.

Here are just a few examples of what employers write in or omit from their offer letters that can negatively impact the value of an employment relationship.

Non-Competes

Many employers will require a one-year non-compete prohibiting you from working with what they refer to as "competitive" or "competing" businesses. Do not be fooled. Get clarity on what this means before you sign. Make the employer define the business for you or narrow the definition further if it seems too broad to you. A seasoned professional working in pharma would never accept "pharma" as a definition of a competitive business. They would narrow it by area or field. They might also carve out working for a non-competitive division or unit of another large pharma company. Nothing damages an employment relationship and ruins a future career more than having your ability to leave a position severely restricted because your options in finding another job are limited by a terrible non-competition agreement. It does not matter whether you think the non-compete is unenforceable. All that matters is what your prospective employer thinks when you share the non-compete with them and they turn you down because they do not want to get involved in the middle of a dispute with your current employer.

We cannot overstate the danger to your career from failing to negotiate or understand your non-compete obligations. Many professionals have remained employed in a dead-end job *much* longer than they should have because the new opportunities conflicted with their non-compete obligations.

Annual Bonus Traps

Almost every employment offer grants the employer the right to cancel your bonus if you are not employed on the date the bonuses are paid. This is a potential disaster in the making. If annual bonuses are paid on December 31 and you are fired on December 30, you forfeit your entire bonus unless you negotiated payment of the bonus despite your termination.

Omissions of Key Terms

Most employers will not include stipulations that may be of extraordinary value to you. These include terms like a salary review at least once per year, eligibility for promotion, or severance, which we cover later in the book.

Lack of Notice Before Terminating Your Employment

Notice is also a carefully negotiated concept and means that the employer has to notify you in advance of the day your employment is ending. This is called a notice period. Because most employment relationships are at-will, employers rarely see a need to provide you with any notice before terminating your employment, although they will ask you for several weeks' notice before you quit to avoid disrupting their business operations. In fact, employers like to fire fast and hire slow to avoid having terminated employees linger at the office for a whole host of reasons, ranging from a concern that they will damage morale or just grouse about their termination. Or they may be concerned about the employee holding onto/copying documents or other company property which is suboptimal for the company.

Needless to say, request as much notice as possible before being fired. It is always easier to look for another job while still employed, and prospective employers prefer professionals who leave voluntarily over those who have been fired or laid off (because it raises less questions about them). Ask your prospective employer for at least thirty days' notice before being terminated. Even if the employer reserves the right to let you go immediately but pay you for the notice period, that is more money in your pocket!

Chapter Four

> The total value of a role is the prize,
> not the offered compensation packages for the role.

CHAPTER FIVE

WHY IS SHARING YOUR SALARY INFORMATION SO DAMAGING TO YOUR CAREER?

"Your paycheck is not your employer's responsibility. Your employer has no control over your value, but you do."

Jim Rohn

What are you making now? The dreaded question of how to express value when asked what you are making remains a pivotal aspect of every employment negotiation. Telling a prospective employer how much you are making is an absolute disaster in employment negotiations because that employer will use your salary information to develop their initial offer and you lose leverage to bargain in the process. Additionally, if you are already underpaid, you will perpetuate that mistake.

Selling Ourselves Short

So why do we disclose this information and allow employers to gain the upper hand when we know how terrible that decision is for our bargaining power? A bad combination of misinformation and doubt about our own value. Fake news in the marketplace leads us to believe that if we do not provide our salary information an employer will never offer us a job, and the fear of missing out on a good job motivates the disclosure. We also routinely question our own value, and that doubt leads us to conclude that our current salary represents a good benchmark of our value.

The problem of salary disclosure has in fact become so pervasive that it has led several states in the US to pass sweeping new laws known as "salary history bans," which preclude employers from directly asking about your current income. But this is not an effective solution. Employers can overcome this legal restriction simply by asking what your salary expectations are and the rationale that drives those expectations. As with everything else we have covered in this book, we need to unpack the misconceptions here and then derive the solution to the problem.

Let us tackle the issue of personal value first. Current salary may be a good internal benchmark for you but does nothing for you in salary negotiations. Think about it this way. How many automobiles have you been able to lease or purchase at cost in your lifetime? The answer is likely none. Even if the sales representative was willing to tell you what the actual cost of making the car is, the answer is irrelevant because the dealership needs to profit from the sale.

You need to profit as well. Your value is constantly increasing as your skills advance, your knowledge increases, and your experience makes you more efficient and effective in your work. Candidly, in this hyper-competitive market, your value in the marketplace would likely increase regardless of your developing career because the demand for good talent perpetually exceeds the supply out there. Employers are always looking for exceptional talent and are willing to pay handsomely for it. So why would you *ever* deliver a static pronouncement of your value in employment negotiations and offer your services at cost? As we have already covered, you are certainly not on sale and should never settle or compromise your value.

Turning the Tables

Knowing that disclosing salary is both unnecessary and a disastrous step in employment negotiations, how do you address the issue when employers insist on needing the information from you?

You change the conversation entirely. This is easier than it sounds. As we discussed in the first chapter, the employer is the buyer of services here and has a definitive view of what they want to offer based on role, experience, fit, and budget. The secret to steering the conversation is knowing that the employer is going to present you with the half-truth that they need your salary information or expectations to determine if you are in the same ballpark compensation-wise.

Once the employer provides its explanation as to why you need to provide the salary information, you ask the employer what salary band the position carries. This is the minimum and maximum the employer is willing to pay for a given job level. Then focus the discussion on the factors that impact the specific compensation the employer offers. Assuming the salary band fits within your compensation needs and expectations, you can focus the discussion on your experience level and advise the employer that the top of the salary band is either in a good range for your discussions or tell them that your expectations exceed the band and explain why that is the case. Getting to a discussion of salary band is necessary, as you need to know if the employer's expectations on compensation are in line with yours. Delaying the inevitable just wastes your valuable time.

If your prospective employer is unwilling or unable to offer a salary band and tries to dismiss the subject as being "entirely subjective" or "discretionary," tell the employer that you will consider all reasonable offers and assume the employer's offer will be based on job level and your experience and expected contributions (basically, "make me your best offer"). If all else fails, you offer a salary range of your own in which your current salary is *below* the range you propose to the employer. Remember, the thrust of the discussion must be about the *position* and engaging the buyer in the purpose and value of the position, and only then frame the discussion about money.

**Rather than tell them what you make,
ask what the employer will pay for your unique value.**

CHAPTER SIX

SHOULD YOU STAY OR SHOULD YOU GO?

> "In a chronically leaking boat, energy devoted to changing vessels is more productive than energy devoted to patching leaks."
>
> *Warren Buffett*

So now we know the true mechanics of employment negotiations, their function and purpose, what we are bargaining for, and how to approach them properly. From here, we move into new roles, learn the ropes and dynamics of the new employer, develop or deliver on our performance requirements and objectives, and actually figure out what we really bargained for in the first place.

But in the course of working in the new role, we invariably come across things we do not like, including the upper limits of the position. Reaching these limits will ultimately force us to grapple with an important decision, borrowing from the immortal song "Should I Stay or Should I Go," written by The Clash in the 1980s.

The irony is that the song's lyrics can be applied to the problem we are examining, and they assess something really important that we explore here:

> *If you go, there will be trouble.*
> *And if you stay, it will be double.*

Many professionals fear change, however, and take comfort in the advice of well-intentioned colleagues or friends that staying in a mediocre position or with a terrible employer cannot harm their careers.

They would be wrong on many levels for holding that belief.

This misconception, more than any other, is one that must be closely examined and quickly dispelled, because it involves career trajectory and has the potential to damage careers more than any other miscalculation about employment relationships. To understand why, we need to understand the mechanics of career trajectory and how our employment decisions become more important as we age.

Time Cuts Both Ways

Our working lives are all about time, the most finite and precious resource we have as human beings. Time spent in each role is valuable in terms of building career experience, but it also costs us. Time also impacts not only how our organizations look at us but also how the marketplace looks at us. Age is most certainly a determining – and, at a certain point, limiting – factor in how our value is assessed.

Employees in their twenties, thirties, and forties are diligently trying to climb the corporate ladder in search of their dream job. These are the years to make connections, garner experience, and learn both the methodology and skill set to position yourself for advancement. Most companies, however, will not give a CEO or

COO position to someone in their early forties unless they are truly extraordinary.[4]

Someone in their fifties or sixties might be more focused on retaining their current position based on concerns that prospective employers will see their age as a liability. This is only the case when you have not developed enough experience or savvy to get higher-level roles. As certain doors close relating to starter or mid-level positions, new ones open. This is why successful senior executives in their fifties or early sixties do not see their age as much of a limiting factor as other professionals. Only through time have they become qualified and thereby highly sought after for officer-level positions or board roles – positions where maturity and experience are crucial for success. Experience and success over time become true leverage for them, provided that they have gained enough of both when opportunity presents itself.

The willingness to hire people later in their respective careers also varies by sector. Software, tech, and biotech companies, for example, are all looking for broad-based experience when hiring. Because those industries are newer, they are looking for employees who can add unique characteristics and depth of experiences that a younger business lacks. Advanced age may be a distinct competitive advantage over hiring younger candidates with less maturity and experience.

---

4   "CHIEF EXECUTIVE OFFICER DEMOGRAPHICS AND STATISTICS IN THE," Zippia, September 9, 2022, https://www.zippia.com/chief-executive-officer-jobs/demographics/

Age Is Not the Problem

While age can be an impediment to a career, the problem is not about getting "old" since we are all aging together. While it is true that some individuals might have an inherent bias against age as a physical characteristic (physical prowess or energy levels), the real issue is that all employees become more costly to businesses as they climb the corporate ladder. Expensive salary and maximized benefits, which companies call "total compensation," might ultimately exceed what the employer is willing or able to afford when they can hire younger and cheaper employees.

When you become too expensive, an employer's choices are to either bear the expense in the budget to justify your package, leading to tension as expectations for ever-increasing performance arise, or find another way to push you out. Employers have become very adept at letting people go without making it appear age based. If they want to move you out, employers can develop a whole litany of reasons to validate their decision; typically, they will use performance reviews to set a tone or a case for taking action. That is why employees need to be alert to the warning signs as they develop and depart before they are let go. If you stay in a role too long, eventually, you will become lackluster in your position whether you know it or not and/or the employer's expectations based on your compensation will outweigh any reasonable performance ability on your part, and you will be fired.

How many times have you heard people say, "I've been doing this too long"?

That mindset means that they most certainly *have* been doing it too long, and this will have a profound impact on their attitude and enthusiasm about work. They might start coming in a bit later or leaving a bit early, believing that they have become so efficient or effective in their position that they do not need to be there all the time. They might start to dread waking up in the morning or find it hard to sleep at night because of intrusive thoughts about job dissatisfaction. When this spills over into family life because of the stress at work, it hits a flashpoint that can affect your whole life, not just your career.

That is when it is time to go – before you are asked to leave. Chances are if you feel this way, someone has already noticed and may be taking steps to end the relationship on the best terms for the employer. And of course, you want to find another job while working for an employer to avoid needing to explain to a new employer that you are currently unemployed.

But there is an important and under-investigated flipside to this problem: *Just as you age in your position, the position itself ages.* Let us delve into what that means.

Experiencing Job Decay

Many of us have had the lightbulb go on in our heads about being too long in a role. That sense that something has faded or worn down in a given position and simply does not feel as vibrant, challenging, or worthwhile as it once was. Those signs or indications confirm that your role has declined in value.

As hard as it is to believe, every job decays in value just like a car. There is no such thing as a job that maintains its value over time. After all, how many active Y2K programmers do you know, assuming you even remember the reference! Of course, you can advance in a job. You can push the boundaries and expand the role. But it is still the same position, and it will not continue holding the same value for you. In fact, if you remain in the same position too long, it may result in your job – and, by extension, *you* – appearing antiquated, obsolete, or worse.

Sounds crazy, right? The employer has not changed the job. You have the same title. Your pay has not varied markedly from what it was. You have the same benefits. That does not sound like the car depreciation analogy, does it? Yes, it does. It is just more subtle, and you do not notice it because, in this analogy, *your job is the car* and it is hard to see what is happening.

Think about it. When you drive a car off a lot, you paid a fixed amount for that car. Once bought or leased, the car no longer has its original retail value, and that number continues to decrease by the day. You can see firsthand how it ages and declines in value. The door gets dinged, the tires need to be replaced, the brakes get squeaky, and so on.

How well you maintain the car and its accrued mileage affects the depreciated value. Eventually, the wear and tear begin to show, the warranty expires, and money needs to be poured into the car just to sustain it. At some point, the car is no longer worth the capital investment, particularly since a new car requires none of that capital outlay. So, as the owner you can trade it in for a new car and walk away. You do not continue throwing resources at a rusty old car.

Every one of these same characteristics applies to job decay in a role. All roles start with unlimited potential. But after a period of time, the grace period (i.e., the "warranty") expires on the position. Ultimately, if you do not or cannot demonstrate to your employer that your value meets or exceeds the scope of the role, you become increasingly vulnerable to termination, like the breakdown of the car. "Environmental conditions," or external factors, and your perspective also adversely affect the job. Over time, the job no longer feels new. You may become complacent or even disinterested in the position, perhaps because you are not learning anything new, and with no training or further advancement possibilities you begin to stagnate. There is "wear and tear" in the role because of business climate, personnel, changes in market conditions, and other critical factors. The job may also "break down" through performance issues, downsizing, budgetary conditions, and so forth. Ultimately, you get to the point where you have gotten as much "mileage" out of the position as possible. And that is when you try to "trade in" your current role for a new position either with your current employer or a prospective one.

While we are performing in a role, we seldom consider the measurement or evaluation of longevity in a role against its lifespan. Thus, it is exceedingly difficult to determine whether we have been in the position too long and if we are suffering from job **depreciation** or decay. We often overlook the immense risk of the position failing us when thinking about the employment relationship. This can include when business relationships become toxic, when the role you accepted is not in reality what you are being asked to do, and when there is career stagnation without any opportunities for growth. If you know what to look for, you can see early signs of stagnation in any role.

Every position, from junior staff to C-suite, has the same characteristics: A *life cycle* that defines the total time you are employed by a given employer from start to finish and a *lifespan* for your role or position. There are four distinct stages of a job lifecycle.

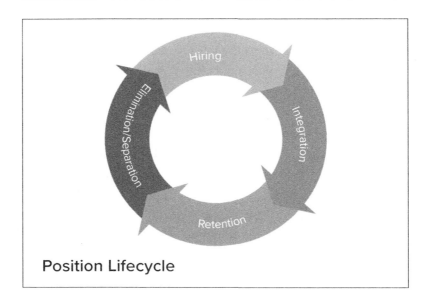

Position Lifecycle

Believe it or not, job decay literally starts from the first day of your job. This is because all those discussions and negotiations you had with an employer about the role and scope of work and cultural values were all based on nothing more than educated and informed guesses you and your employer had about what it would be like to work together. Reality may be very different than the fantasy of the job you or your employer had in mind. The decay rate may also increase gradually or quickly with each successive stage of the life cycle depending on the problems you encounter in each stage. The more pronounced the problems or issues in each stage, the more likely that the decay accelerates.

Stage One: Hiring
The hiring stage is typically the first thirty to sixty days of employment. To what extent decay occurs in this stage depends upon how closely your expectations about the position align with your employer's expectations about your fit in the position. Unfortunately, in many employment instances, professionals find themselves

"buying a lemon." Just like the car you buy that looks fantastic but has been back in the repair shop three times this month, your shiny new position can be very different from what you thought you were getting yourself into, and the differences are typically not good ones (or worse, are very unpleasant surprises).

Welcome to the problem of "alignment," the assessment of job fit for a given position. Alignment can only be assessed after the job starts, which explains why it is the make-or-break problem everyone experiences during the hiring stage.

Examples of these alignment issues are everywhere, and you likely have experienced them firsthand. For instance, your employer told you in the interview process or negotiation stage about their wonderful and collaborative work environment (really, would an employer ever say otherwise?), but then you arrive to find a combative work environment with toxic team members and tone-deaf management. Your friend shares that her supervisor is a narcissist who presented himself as charming and personable during the interview process (which all narcissists do, by the way) but now working with this person is an unexpected challenge.

Stage Two: Integration
This is the **onboarding** stage, one of the two phases in which most of the decay and failure occurs.

What is integration or onboarding and why is it so impactful to job decay? Professionals and employers have confused orientation with onboarding for decades. Orientation lasts only a few days and consists of meetings that give you a broad overview of how things work at your new employer and completing all the new hire paperwork. In contrast, onboarding is a process that takes up to twelve to eighteen months, during which time the employer helps you get up to speed in the role, absorb the culture and values of the organization, and so on.[5]

Relationships decline or can outright fail during onboarding because employment relationships require time, attention, and maintenance – three things in short supply with badly managed organizations. It is therefore not surprising that failure happens here with remarkable frequency. According to Inc. Magazine, a startling 86 percent of employees leave their positions *within six months absent effective onboarding*.[6] Job decay relating to onboarding issues happens very quickly and includes factors like lack of communication and establishment of core priorities and objectives that the employer expects you to fulfill in your new role or position. Lack of goal setting, feedback, measurement of success in a role, and integration of a diverse workforce is the responsibility of the employer, and if they ignore these issues during onboarding, employees rapidly lose enthusiasm, drive, and professional development within the organization. Employees can also fail employers in the onboarding stage. If you do not show interest as an active participant and show initiative in helping to set goals for yourself in the absence of guidance, you will be looked at as disengaged.

---

5   "Create an Exceptional Onboarding Journey For Your New Employees," Gallup, n.d., https://www.gallup.com/workplace/247076/onboarding-new-employees-perspective-paper.aspx

6   Marcel Schwantes, "Research Says 86 Percent of Employees Quit Within the First Six Months, Unless Managers Do These 4 Things," Inc., December 13, 2017, https://www.inc.com/marcel-schwantes/good-managers-practice-this-1-masterful-strategy-to-make-sure-new-employees-dont-quit.html

Set and develop your own goals and initiatives just as you likely mapped out in the interview process. Passivity does not work here and can engender a perception of you as a follower rather than a leader. Furthermore, disengagement rapidly accelerates decay.

Stage Three: Retention

The **retention** stage is the second of the two phases in which job decay and failure frequently accelerate. Retention describes the rate at which employers keep consistent, long-term employees. We prefer to think of it as the active involvement of both you and your employer to demonstrate an interest in your continued employment with the organization. Retention depends on many key factors, including:

- Mutual trust and respect.
- Collaboration.
- Training and education.
- Leadership and mentorship programs.
- Frequent informal reviews, check-ins, and feedback.
- Development of advancement or promotion tracks.
- Compensation and benefits growth and development (e.g., raises, better health care coverage, gym or auto allowance perks).

The moment when either you or your employer no longer demonstrate continued interest in your position is when alignment fails and decay gets progressively worse.

Stage Four: Elimination or Separation

The obvious end stage of any employment lifecycle. This is the point at which the continuation of your role is no longer sustainable for either you or for your employer and one of you takes action. By this stage, you have experienced accelerated decay through each prior stage, and you have reached a tipping point – the point of no return.

The end of life for a position is inevitable, even if you obtain the exact job you bargained for. Your existing role will only benefit your growth and development up to a certain point before needing to be course corrected, supplemented, or abandoned altogether to keep your career on track.

The onset of this stage involves a conscious decision by you or your employer that the position has run its course for whatever reason. Whether it is decline in mutual interest or the benefits of the relationship or changing financial constraints or needs, you or your employer have reached the conclusion that you need to quit or be fired.

Professionals have come to describe arriving at this stage as hitting an invisible wall and expecting it to move, only to realize that it never will. The secret is to stay ahead of the curve to offer a value proposition that always exceeds what it costs to employ you. You instinctively know this to be true based on your career experience.

Factors Impacting the Rate of Job Decay

Now that you are familiar with job decay, you should know the rate of decay depends on two dynamic forces: the laws of **depreciation** and **diminishing returns**. These are two compelling principles of accounting and economics that best explain what happens to a given position over time. Diminishing returns applies to employees and their efforts in a role, and depreciation applies to the role itself.

The law of diminishing returns is a well-stated principle that means that after a certain point, your efforts in connection with an activity, your ongoing work or investment in that activity produces smaller improvements or results.

Consider this example: In 1926, Henry Ford made national headlines by cutting his factory workers' hours to no more than 40 hours per week during a five-day work week (reduced from six days per week). By allowing his employees to have reliable time for rest and relaxation with family or to pursue their personal interests, Ford reaped a tremendous windfall of increased productivity per hour. He was absolutely correct, as the fresher and more motivated employees produced more per hour than their overworked counterparts. Anything above that 40-hour threshold and their units per hour actually fell, hence the "diminishing" in diminishing returns. As an added bonus, the workers became fiercely loyal to Ford, resulting in decreased turnover. The bottom line is that diminishing returns assumes that putting in more hours at work does not mean we actually get more accomplished and impacts career trajectory.

Suppose you are in the same job, with the same manager, with similar daily challenges, and so forth. No matter what effort you put into the job, it is extremely unlikely that your efforts will lead to marked growth or development in that job *after a certain point in time*. There is no trick or gimmick to overcoming diminishing returns, of course. If you can advance, get additional training or mentorship, or find new opportunities with your employer, the rate of decay will likely slow down. If you are promoted to a new position by your current employer, decay may reset and start all over again. However, the decay rate might also increase more rapidly than it otherwise would in the new job because you are still within the same ecosystem with the same people.

But make no mistake. Positions *never* regain their original value or "new car smell." You can improve or slow the decay rate depending on how the position evolves or as you advance. But the role diminishes in career value all the same. Effectively, roles are in an inverse relationship to time because the more time spent in a role, the less value it has to a career. And as we get older, fewer opportunities materialize unless we have the growth and development to support career advancement, which never happens by staying in a role too long.

This brings us to the other variable impacting job value: depreciation. At a high level, depreciation simply means that the value of certain kinds of capital goes down over time. To combat depreciation, we care for our assets to maximize their lifespan. If we want our car to continue to run efficiently and for the maximum time possible, we change the oil and repair dents or dings before they are allowed to rust and decay. It is safe to say that many people spend more time and energy combating the depreciation of their cars than their careers. In our employment-centric focus, depreciation indicates the declining value of the role and of your compensation over time – and potentially the increased opportunity cost of remaining in that depreciating role. Many people do not consider the fact that the role itself is losing value over time because they neglect the need to grow and develop beyond it. This is the dynamic tension. The reason we need advancement or promotion is that we outgrow our role. Remaining in that role has great value to the employer (no need to train replacements, stagnating wages, job expertise, etc.) but has decreasing value to you over time.

Consider this: If your compensation does not materially increase from year to year, you are losing wage value. Inflation is a primary factor. Your salary does not go as far this year as last year because the prices of goods and services you consume increase while your salary stays static. If your raise does not exceed the rate of inflation, it will feel like a pay cut. A raise for excellent performance that does not outpace inflation is simply not a raise. In effect, you are losing money year over year. Add to that intrinsic economic pressures like the fact that your value in the marketplace continues to increase, but you are not reaping that reward, and the result is a further reduction in the value of your compensation. If you maintain the same position without compensation adjustment, even at the **cost-of-living adjustment (COLA)** level, your cost of living impacts your compensation value.

A role is similar. Over time, roles decay. Without advancement opportunity and support, proper management and direction, supervision, mentoring, and training (typically employer-sponsored activities) the value of a role will diminish over time. There are a variety of reasons why this occurs: overlapping positions (two positions in a business with similar responsibilities), reduction in role scope because of organizational changes, and loss of team members or support systems. Your age also plays a factor as you become too expensive for the role, and so your particular value in the role decays for your employer as well.

This is a graph of what depreciation looks like. Asset Value is the inverse of Time. Careers can decay more slowly or more rapidly than straight line or fixed depreciation because of intervening circumstances or conditions.

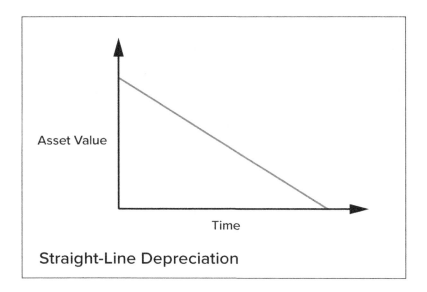

Straight-Line Depreciation

The severity of the decay, or "decay rate," can increase for a whole variety of reasons: reduction in job scope, performance decline, personality conflicts with superiors, internalizing workplace issues creating social or personal issues, and so forth. Decay rate can also decrease for a variety of reasons as well, such as role expansion or advancement, new training opportunities, a new and improved boss, a reduction in conflicts between co-workers, and so forth.

Over time, no matter what occurs in a given role, your efforts will have diminishing results. Then the role itself will have diminishing or decaying value to you and, ultimately, the organization. If this does not result in your termination, it will certainly lead to stagnation, unhappiness, or dissatisfaction and likely inform your own decision to depart.

You will undoubtedly recognize this feeling as you work. You feel like you are performing well but working too hard for your given results or accolades. That feeling spills over when you return home, causing stress in your home environment, including relationships and sleep patterns. Trouble in these areas will carry over to your attitude and demeanor the next workday, solidifying a vicious cycle that can be extremely destructive to your job and your family. This cycle will continually repeat and eventually form a death spiral where the job decay reaches the point of no return, as does your position. You need to get ahead of the problem before the cycle can take hold and ruin what you have worked so hard to achieve.

Managing Your Trajectory

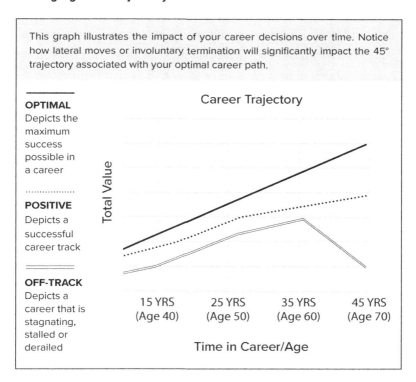

This chart graphically depicts career trajectory or Lifetime Career Value™(LCV). LCV measures where an individual stands over the course of career based upon two important concepts:

- Total Value of your career (TV) as the X axis.
- Time in Career (TC) as the Y axis.

TV is based upon the value of your role and compensation. TC measures the number of years you have devoted to working in your career over time. Viewed this way, LCV explains that career success is all about maximizing TV while minimizing the opportunity costs and risks of forfeiture, such as job loss or resignation, experienced during TC.

The solid line represents or reflects a perfect trajectory – increasingly better positions or advancement over time. In case you are concerned that your career does not look like the solid line, you are in good company. Most of us do not have trajectories like this, but it is aspirational. That is what a perfect or close-to-perfect trajectory looks like for comparative purposes. The dotted line reflects a positive real-world scenario, with mostly positive career moves: an employee who receives a major promotion at age 40, changes positions to VP at age 43, becomes SVP at age 52, and ultimately becomes a C-suite executive in his or her sixties.

The double line reflects a negative real-world scenario, complete with missteps, poorly considered lateral moves, and stagnation: an employee who experiences sudden job loss at age 62, rushes to accept a comparable position and salary in a different industry where a lack of experience proves to be the employee's undoing, and an inability to perform well in the role. This is happening across the country today.

We sell ourselves short, leap into poorly thought-out roles, switch industries or change careers entirely, experience matters out of our control that require taking extended leave from work, position eliminations, or other unexpected adversities during employment. These issues create deceleration, deflection, or reduction in our career trajectory.

Everyone is inevitably going to experience a dip in trajectory for one reason or another. We are not trying for a perfect career; that does not exist. The goal is to be aware, look for opportunities, and be purposeful in the changes you make. At the same time, we want to make sure that every career change is positively impactful and stays parallel or close to that optimal 45-degree angle. To borrow a concept from the artist John W. Gardner, careers, much like life, represent the art of "drawing without an eraser" because you can never go back, only move forward. On many occasions, unfortunately, career climbers make impulsive decisions motivated by fear, uncertainty, and doubt, and their career derailleurs accelerate as they compound the problem with every misstep.

Over time, as the gap widens between potential and actual value of your career, it becomes increasingly difficult to stay close to that line because experience over time becomes a significant factor in determining what positions are available to you as we discussed earlier in this chapter. Certain doors will close (jobs you are overqualified for by experience and cost), and others will open, provided you have enough experience to qualify for them.

The only way to keep your career as close to the solid line as possible is to remain vigilant in assessing our remaining job value, managing and preventing career decay, and wisely choosing new opportunities. This takes dedicated effort and a good coach, but do not skip to the last chapter now! You need to look at your career in a whole new way, continuously assessing when you need to move to better positions.

Let us start with the reasons *why* we need to be evaluating career moves every few years.

According to a 2018 study from the United States Bureau of Labor Statistics, the public repository of all information regarding workforce dynamics in the United States, employees typically do not remain in a position for more than four years. There is a value proposition in a role for a finite period of time, and the sweet spot is *four years or less* in a given position to ensure positive career advancement.[7] For some, particularly those in service occupations, the average time they remain in given positions is half of the national average.

There are many reasons why we remain in positions for such a short period of time, including the need for better training and growth opportunities. The motivated among us quickly realize as they develop in our careers that progression and advancement will ultimately not be found without moving on to better positions. We also learn that our ability to make more money depends on career mobility. Just like taking the first offer can damage your earning potential (covered in the next chapter), so does remaining in a static position (i.e., a position with little to no advancement opportunity) for more than five years. In fact, the ability to earn greatly depends on the speed of advancement.

---

7   Alison Doyle, "How Long Should an Employee Stay at a Job?" The Balance, August 12, 2021, https://www.thebalancemoney.com/how-long-should-an-employee-stay-at-a-job-2059796.

Race to the C-Suite

In 2018, *Harvard Business Review* published a fascinating decade-long study on the factors that contributed to certain professionals becoming CEOs as quickly as they did. In this CEO Genome Project, researchers obtained a data set of 17,000 C-suite executives and took a subset of roughly 2,600 to review in earnest. They determined that, on average, someone who became CEO attained this position within an average of twenty-four years from their first job. Using this subset, they identified what they brilliantly labeled "CEO sprinters," or professionals who achieved CEO status in less than the average twenty-four years.

The researchers identified three specific "catapults" that propelled the sprinters to CEO glory: moving back to move forward, taking big risks, and inheriting a big mess that they were able to overcome.[8]

> We discovered a striking finding: Sprinters don't accelerate to the top by acquiring the perfect pedigree. They do it by making bold career moves over the course of their career that catapult them to the top. We found that three types of career catapults were most common among the sprinters. Ninety-seven percent of them undertook at least one of these catapult experiences, and close to 50% had at least two. (In contrast, only 24% had elite MBAs.)

Through these career catapults, executives build the specific behaviors that set successful CEOs apart – including decisiveness,

---

[8] Elena Lytkina Botelho, Kim Rosenkoetter Powell, and Nicole Wong, "The Fastest Path to the CEO Job, According to a 10-Year Study," Harvard Business Review, January 31, 2018, https://hbr.org/2018/01/the-fastest-path-to-the-ceo-job-according-to-a-10-year-study.

reliability, adaptability, and the ability to engage for impact – and they get noticed for their accomplishments. The catapults are so powerful that even people in our study who never aspired to become CEO ultimately landed the position by pursuing one or more of these strategies.

The sprints referenced in the study are completely on point. The three archetypes for that article were the people who traveled lesser-known and riskier paths and were able to launch themselves ahead in their careers and ahead of the competition. The CEO sprinters created opportunity from nothing, challenged themselves by taking extreme risks with their own career trajectory, or took on and resolved a legacy issue. In each case, these sprinters likely realized that time was of the essence and they needed to move themselves to the next stage of their careers.

The key takeaways from this research against the backdrop of our trajectory chart confirm that the most successful careers come from maximizing effort and advancement to get ahead of the limitations that arise when you stay too long in given roles.

Here is an example of how stagnating in a role can limit everything that matters to you about your career: A company employs you as its shiny new VP of sales and marketing at $150,000 a year. You think this is fantastic because your last employer only paid you $125,000 as a senior director. You now have a more marketable position for future advancement and are making considerably more money to boot. So, what is the catch?

Your role has already begun to decay.

Flash forward two years. You are still VP of sales and marketing. During that two-year period, you received no salary increase in the first year and only a 2 percent increase in the following year. When you research the amount companies are willing to pay for your position, you discover the problem. Your competitors are willing to pay between $175,000 and $200,000 for new hires in your current position. That is $25,000 to $50,000 more in the pocket of someone who presumably has significantly less experience than you do in your role!

Attracting New Talent by Any Means Necessary

Smart business owners know that to attract or steal new talent, they need to have competitive compensation packages. This generally means an upward salary adjustment to entice prospective hires.

The same is simply not as true for companies managing the compensation needs of internal hires. These days, a 7 percent raise is about the most you can reasonably expect to receive in annual salary increases unless you acquire promotional opportunities or a new job (14.8 percent).[9] This explains why changing jobs every three to five years is extremely beneficial and promotes career trajectory with greater earning potential and a broader base of skills. Current employers often cannot or will not compete with the package given to a new hire.

Yet there is another compelling reason why we need to change jobs over time: perception of the marketplace about you. *Forbes* wrote a series of truly compelling articles about the potential damage to

---

9 "WHAT IS THE AVERAGE ANNUAL RAISE IN THE US?" Zippia, July 10, 2022, https://www.zippia.com/advice/average-annual-raise/.

your career by remaining in static roles.[10] The bottom line is that if you stay longer than three to five years in a role that does not involve senior leadership or big, juicy promotions, the market perception is that you are disinterested or unmotivated or that you have grown complacent in your career. Otherwise, why would you stay so long in current or past positions? Those are the questions a recruiter or prospective employer will be pondering when they review your LinkedIn profile or resume. There is absolutely no reason to remain in a position with no real potential for growth.

You Are Not the Only Party Assessing Value

This is another critical reason to switch positions, and it is one that professionals often overlook. While employers may appreciate your continued development in your role, ultimately, employers value one thing above all else: return on investment (ROI). The duration of your employment greatly depends upon the ROI you are offering your employer at any given time.

ROI is defined as a measure of the difference delta between the cost of an asset and its increase in value over time. The stock market is all about ROI. If you purchased a significant amount of Apple stock on July 8, 1982, when it was at its historic low of $0.04 per share, you would be wildly wealthy today. That is because you invested in the stock when it was at a low price and can now sell it for a much higher price, netting an enormous return on your investment.

---

10   Liz Ryan, "Ten Ways It Hurts You to Stay In One Job Too Long," Forbes, August 30, 2016, https://www.forbes.com/sites/lizryan/2016/08/30/ten-ways-it-hurts-you-to-stay-in-one-job-too-long/?sh=7a17d9c741b6.

In terms of your value to your company, ROI is how much profit or loss you have created for the company. The company invests in you by way of your salary, health care benefits, paid vacation, and the like. It wants to ensure that you contribute enough value to the company's bottom line to justify your cost. It is also looking to see if someone can do the same or similar work as you for a lesser cost. If you have become too expensive, and the company can get someone into your position with a lower salary, it will do so to maximize the ROI on your position for the company. If you have proven your worth, the company may also move you into a more advanced role with better compensation terms and conditions.

Let us take a look at an example. If you spend five or six years in a role, while you are likely quite accomplished at that role, you have also likely become more expensive in that role thanks to salary raises, perhaps even exceeding the top of the salary band for that position. Your employer is paying you more in that role than they could pay your replacement. That replacement might perform at a somewhat lower level than you while still meeting the position's requirements. When you stay in the role too long, you get replaced because your value diminishes in the role while your carrying costs go up. In the market, they can replace you with a cheaper alternative. As an aside, promoting you to a position more commensurate with your salary may also not be the solution because your employer may perceive that you are not ready for an advanced role and simply let you go.

What happens next is obvious. The employer will replace you if there is no place to put you where your ROI continues to grow because you have become too expensive for your role. In other words, your ROI diminishes to the point that keeping you employed does not make sense for your employer and your situation will end.

So, no matter what lens we use to evaluate ongoing relationships, the result is the same: *Your position has limited value over time and will damage your trajectory if you remain in it too long.* You have to continue to improve your value, and that might require you to leave your current employer to do so.

Getting Ahead Rather than Lagging Behind Is a Must

So now you know why you must advance internally or move jobs every few years. The trick is appreciating the need for job change and acting upon it in an effective and informed way. You *must* anticipate the need for job change for two very important reasons:

- The time involved in finding a new job.
- The impact of losing a job while looking for one.

The time it takes to locate and secure new employment is considerable. The average job search takes two to four months to secure a given position, with executive positions taking more than four months.[11] Now imagine you are looking for a great new position while under pressure, whether it is a rapidly declining position, fear of job loss, or actually losing your current job. Nothing derails careers faster than time out of work or rushing job selection, which can lead to accepting poorly negotiated great jobs or lateral or inferior ones. Yet these situations become inevitable for any

---

11 Tim Madden, "Why It Takes So Long To Land A Job, Especially For Executives," Forbes, February 15, 2022, https://www.forbes.com/sites/forbescoachescouncil/2022/02/15/why-it-takes-so-long-to-land-a-job-especially-for-executives/.

professional who takes their eyes off of their career management. Remaining vigilant in managing your growth and development will make the difference between a career with sustained growth and success and one that lags behind.

> Every position has a lifespan, just like a car.
> Do not stay until the warranty has expired!

CHAPTER SEVEN

SHOULD YOU TAKE IT OR LEAVE IT?

> "You accepted less because you thought
> a little was better than nothing.
> Know your worth."
>
> *Trent Shelton*

So, you have made the decision to change employers. The writing is on the wall, your role has decayed to the point of no return, and you find a great new opportunity. This is another critical point in career trajectory when many professionals fail to effectively utilize their leverage and negotiate a better offer than they receive from their prospective employers.

So how impactful is accepting the first offer? If you projected this decision out over an entire career – to consistently say yes to the first offer – with a job starting at $90,000 a year over forty-five years without negotiated increases of at least 5 percent per move, you would likely lose out on wage increases in excess of $1,500,000.

You are literally leaving money on the table. And who can afford to lose that kind of money? Never, ever take the first offer.

Ironically, this reactive decision-making can be more damaging to your career than remaining in the existing role. No matter how much trajectory you have lost in the current position, you compound the problem if you make a move and trade away the increased value of that new position. This will damage the optimal trajectory of your career from that position forward because you failed to improve the value of that position in the negotiation process.

You have not just harmed your earning potential in this role; you have now compromised the earning potential of your subsequent jobs as well. This initial misstep compounds itself over the span of your career.

If you have experienced this in your career, you are not alone. A 2018 job seeker survey conducted by ZipRecruiter[12] found that a whopping 64 percent of job seekers accepted the first salary offer without negotiation the last time they were hired. Younger respondents were more likely than their older counterparts to take the first offer. But even among participants aged forty-five to fifty-four, with more work experience under their belts, a stunning 59 percent said they accepted the first salary offer they received.

Women engaged in this behavior more frequently than men and minorities overall. A sizable number of female professionals have shared with us a very specific fear that precludes them from negotiating effectively. It is not a fear that employers will refuse to counter their counteroffer. Rather, they fear that employers will pull the offer altogether. We have not heard many men express this same fear. This fear can, unfortunately, stack the deck against women before they even sign the dotted line for a new position.

---

12 "The ZipRecruiter 2018 Annual Job Seeker Survey," ZipRecruiter, December 13, 2018, https://www.ziprecruiter.com/blog/ziprecruiter-2018-annual-job-seeker-survey/.

The most startling part of this revelation is that many professionals do not even know they have the option to negotiate or consciously choose not to engage in that process. Some do not want to be perceived as difficult, so they accept without negotiation. Others are in such financial dire straits they feel like they cannot risk losing the offer and jump on it. No matter the rationale, the damage is the same.

Fixing the Problem Requires Another Critical Mindset Shift

So how can we change this dynamic of not negotiating job offers to one where smart negotiating is the key to successful careers? According to the *Harvard Business Review* article, "How to Close the Gender Gap":

> Companies can level the playing field by providing clear information. An online recruiting platform for engineers completely eliminated the gender salary gap for new hires simply by listing the median salary for every position. Before this change, women asked for lower annual salaries than men – more than $4,000 lower, on average. When candidates were presented with the median data, the salaries requested actually equalized.[13]

A job offer is so much more than just the salary offer. As such, there is always a way to improve a job opportunity. There are ways to improve the scope of the role. There are ways to improve the compensation or the compensation opportunity. Lastly, there

---

13   Colleen Ammerman and Boris Groysberg, "How to Close the Gender Gap," Harvard Business Review, May-June 2021, https://hbr.org/2021/05/how-to-close-the-gender-gap.

are ways to diminish or minimize what we call **post-employment restrictions**.

Remember our discussion on ROI? The employer has zero incentive to offer anything more than what they believe the market would require them to pay, and savvy employers are always looking for a bargain. The fact that you are being courted for a position speaks volumes already of the employer's interest in you. It is not that they do not want to bargain. You have to give them the right incentive or leverage them to do so and still be able to justify your package to the company.

Every day, employees negotiate against themselves because they may not know what to ask for. If an employer offers a base salary and does not offer a bonus, sign-on bonus, or equity, you could be sacrificing over 50 percent to 70 percent of the total value of the compensation over the lifetime of the agreement. You need to not only negotiate the elements presented; you also need to know which elements were left out and capitalize on those as well. Worse still, you could inadvertently land a position with less total compensation value than what you currently have, particularly if you are repaying bonuses or losing the value of unvested stock at your existing company upon your departure. That situation is happening all the time today. Professionals fail to read the initial agreement or forget to factor in those types of penalties when making the choice to leave. They often don't ask the new employer to compensate them for money they are losing when they leave their current position. So why do we make the assumption that employers will not play ball?

Employers bargain all day and night. In fact, throughout thirty years in this business, we have only seen employers pull offers on the first counteroffer *once* (and the employer was extremely irrational and unreasonable in dealing with the employee). Even counteroffers that sought a 30 percent to 40 percent compensation increase did not lead to the employer pulling the offer as long as there was a compelling rationale with supporting data. Without building a narrative, you are negotiating from an uninformed posture, which does not benefit any aspect of your negotiating.

You Trade Away Value Every Time You Bet Against Yourself

So how do you negotiate effectively? How do you discover the value you bring to a new employer? And how do you avoid the lack of confidence in the process to assert yourself effectively and maximize your value in those negotiations?

You start by taking the emotion out of the process and keep it from directing or limiting your actions in career negotiations.

First and foremost, you need to drop the fear, uncertainty and doubt as well as the feeling of missing out. As mentioned earlier, these factors are very real, acutely felt, and extremely frustrating, especially for women and minorities. In the aforementioned article featured in *Harvard Business Review,* authors Colleen Ammerman and Boris Groysberg contend that

> Gender-based compensation disparities often start before an employee is actually hired. When the terms and parameters of a salary negotiation are vague, women consistently end up with lower starting pay than men, even when controlling for other relevant factors. By contrast, when women learn that an offer is negotiable, they negotiate as often as men do.

This fear is an insidious by-product of the conditioning many female professionals have faced in their careers to take whatever is offered to them and just be thankful to receive whatever they can get. Many of the women we have worked with have shared with us that they tend to negotiate from a position of insecurity and self-doubt until they think that the space is somehow safe enough to express themselves. Here is how one of our clients, a thirty-year veteran in the pharmaceutical industry at a Fortune 500 company, described her experience with this phenomenon:

> Fear and desperation are powerful derailers in negotiations. Looking back now, I know I should not have allowed them to undermine the obligation I have to myself to be fully valued. Ten years ago, I lost my job. Two weeks prior, my husband lost his job as a partner at a Wall Street firm. We had two children in private school, two elderly mothers to care for, and no idea how long it would take to land on our feet.
>
> I was on the path to VP, responsible for strategy for multiple functions across North America. I had a wonderful team of thirty professionals. My departure was decided swiftly after I declined unequivocally to carry out unethical strategies my boss asked me to execute. While I didn't question my decision to say no, my confidence was crushed. As a Black female in her late forties, my anxiety was debilitating.
>
> My husband was fully supportive of my objection at work since we are both highly principled. To shield us from added pressure, we hid the issue from our mothers, our children, and other family members. I fired up my network, but layoffs were sweeping my industry. Weeks of no prospects felt like months. The most valuable part of our jobless time together

was a chance to take stock of our lives. We decided that our hectic life was unsustainable. He'd retire early, manage the kids and the house, and I'd go full throttle for a VP role.

Fortunately, eight weeks later I found myself in the midst of interviews for an amazing job at one of the largest companies in my field. It was a newly created role, called "Global Strategy Lead" and I was assured it was leveled at Senior Director – a lateral move. The offer letter came with a surprise – the job was leveled at Director, a demotion for me. Given the context at home, I accepted the offer with only one change – vacation time. I was terrified that my offer would be rescinded if I pushed for the title or more money. I was now the breadwinner and felt the weight of all of the people who relied financially on us. I could not take that risk, no matter how illogical it was.

It didn't take long for me to be promoted and for me to land on the high potential radar. I thrived, and I am now known globally for my expertise and am highly regarded across the industry. But I've never recovered the money I left on the table. If I had to do it again, I would have put forth a strong business case for the appropriate level given the complexity and breadth of responsibilities. I would have countered for more in base and a larger signing bonus. I would have had more courage and confidence. I would have been more open with my network because they would have helped with benchmark data. I know fear is real, but it should be separated from what we need to do to be valued. Our value needs to be fully rewarded.

That vignette beautifully encapsulates why women are capable of negotiating effectively once they overcome the fear, which is all psychological although it feels incredibly real. Imagine what our client's career would have been like if she had been able to realize or capture the value lost because of mindset.

This is not to say that men do not suffer from having the wrong mindset about their value. While fear does not seem to be as great an impediment to men advancing in their careers, many male professionals we have worked with suffer from a different emotional distraction: overconfidence. They suffer from the misconception that they know their value so well – or worse, that it will be immediately recognized by their prospective employer – that they can make asks without a compelling rationale or supporting narrative. This is a disastrous error in negotiation. Any approach that comes across as overconfident will place you on a path of receiving suboptimal offers or worse, not receiving offers at all.

This is a nice segue to the next part of this discussion. Replacing emotion with fact. When it comes to how easily we trade away our value, we often engage in negotiations that truly have no meaning because only the employer has done their homework about what a given position is worth. Developing a network of professionals to assist you on this journey is critical. Including recruiters and compensation coaches is a start to get a baseline or perspective as to what positions are worth out there. You need to develop the data points and collect the information before you engage in negotiation. Until you have actually done your homework, how do you know your worth? We have a particular suggestion in this regard, which appears in the conclusion to this book.

Finally, do the research on your target, as previously discussed. Evaluate the salary band or range for the position, get a sense of regional value, and get information about the potential employer where you can through sites like Comparably.com.

You are an achiever seeking even more greatness.
Do not settle for fine.

CHAPTER EIGHT

ARE THERE WAYS TO PROTECT YOURSELF FROM GETTING FIRED?

"I am not a product of my circumstances.
I am a product of my decisions."

Stephen Covey

Another fundamental misconception about employment relationships is that the risk of failure of the relationship rests solely on your shoulders. Again, that is a *buyer* mentality, not a seller mentality. Sellers should know the value of what they are selling.

As we now know, employers frame employment offers or agreements around flexibility and convenience. Therefore, they look to place all of the relationship risk solely on your shoulders. Being able to end the employment relationship when it suits their purpose is really what at-will employment means. Just because employment is at-will does not mean that you cannot rebalance the risk of the relationship in an employment negotiation. In fact, there are powerful risk mitigation tools available to you to do just that!

Think like an employer. Employers always operate from a cost and a risk assessment when it comes to retaining employees. A cost assessment weighs your value as an employee against the expense of continuing your employment. A risk assessment concerns the potential liability to the employer of firing you (e.g., claims filed against the employer like wrongful termination, discrimination, or retaliation). If your cost exceeds your value (remember that discussion on ROI in Chapter 6), your performance declines or actually hurts the company by damaging its reputation or customer relationships, etc., you can move from asset to liability quickly and become a prime candidate for termination.

Professionals often make the mistake of thinking that the only thing they can do to keep themselves from being fired is to make sure their performance exceeds their cost. This is a fundamental misunderstanding. Remember what we said about risk assessment? The risk goes both ways here. If an employer decides to terminate you, it is because first, they no longer see you as an asset and second, they have weighed the liabilities of terminating you and decided that you pose no risk or threat to the organization should they do so. Thus, another way to give you greater job security is to give your employer reason to believe there *are* risks and consequences to terminating your employment so they are reluctant to do so.

Here are a few important employment strategies that can make those risks or consequences a reality and help to protect your interests to boot. The catch is that you must have leverage to obtain them, and all leverage comes from planning in advance. As the saying goes, "Begin with the end in mind!"

Documentation Is Your Best Friend

Staying ahead of a decision to terminate your employment can be one of the most effective methods of preventing involuntary termination. Accordingly, the most powerful form of leverage and the best preventative measure to involuntary termination is your own documentation of your performance. Why is documentation so important? Employers almost always follow specific predetermined processes before termination. Generally speaking, they will document performance issues and use them as a basis to warrant or justify termination. You need to document your performance as well, particularly when you begin to sense a problem.

If you are honest with yourself, you will see what is happening in the demeanor of your superiors and take immediate action. Be proactive! As soon as you see the warning signs take these important steps:

- Get a career coach from outside the company to help you see your role in what is happening.
- Be an active, engaged participant in all communications about your performance and make sure to communicate your side of things *effectively* and *positively*.
- Ensure that there is a formal or informal record of how you resolved or addressed any issues about performance.
- Be open to accepting negative feedback and be prepared to embrace your superior's point of view where it is not costly to do so.
- Provide meaningful feedback on reviews. Assertively (but not aggressively or defensively) challenge the review. Seek to understand the themes and elements behind the feedback received.
- Ask Human Resources (HR) for assistance in resolving disputes or negative issues once you have gotten beyond the point of being able to resolve them yourself.

Get ahead of the train coming off the tracks, because the first thing HR does when evaluating the risk of terminating you is determine whether you have built a case that contradicts what management is telling HR. Always multitask the problem: Begin the process of looking for a new position as soon as you begin to see things souring in your current position. It never hurts to have an exit plan yourself.

In fact, enlisting HR's support in worst-case scenarios might give you an exit strategy before termination occurs. Whatever you do, be honest. Inventing or embellishing issues just to stay employed is the *wrong* way to stay employed and will ultimately lead to an untenable employment situation. If you approach HR openly and honestly, demonstrate that you are receptive to constructive feedback and seek true guidance, you will find a far more welcoming and receptive audience. Conversely, an aggressive or combative posture with HR never works. You will quickly lose credibility and no longer receive the benefit of the doubt that anyone but you caused the issues you are experiencing on the job.

Lock in Your Severance Package

Severance is the payment of compensation and/or benefits on termination. This concept has been misunderstood for years by employees as simply a way to cover the period between positions, but this is a short-sighted interpretation. Although severance might provide time to allow you to cover your expenses while searching for a position, that is not the true value of severance. In reality, severance is the best deterrent to keep a savvy employer from firing you, provided that the cost is high enough to make your employer think twice.

Real world example: You are making $250,000 a year. If your employer is required only to pay you a month of severance, it is worth it to your employer to let you go. There is a small amount of compensation involved. Now imagine your severance is half a year or a year. Now the stakes of terminating you are more significant. An employer will give careful consideration to letting you go with the knowledge that they need to pay out $125,000 to do so. Payments of amounts like that draw attention from upper management, and they will ponder if it is worth it to the company to terminate your employment. Having been involved on the management side in those decisions, we can tell you that this matters – and it works.

Severance can actually be a powerful risk mitigation tool if properly negotiated with that purpose in mind. The larger the severance package, the less likely that the company would terminate employment without cause. The worst thing an employer can imagine is paying an employee to leave when the money spent has no benefit whatsoever to the company.

Here are some important issues about severance that every employee must understand to negotiate severance properly.

Should the Number of Months of Severance Be Equal to the Duration of Non-compete Agreements?
Generally, no. The reason is that compensation is at an all-time high. Back in the 1980s or 1990s, we had C-suites that were making $200,000 a year, and we typically saw one-year non-competes and one-year severances. Now that annual salaries for *VP-level* positions and above routinely exceed those salary figures, we are finding that many employers are not willing to offer employees at that level more than six months of severance yet still expect at least a one-year non-compete period. You should still bargain with your employer if possible to have the severance period and the non-compete period be the same (including in a worst case scenario reducing the non-compete period). If the non-compete you signed really prevents you from getting a great new job for a full year, six months of severance payments will seem like nothing when it ends and you are still out of work.

Do You Recommend Salary Continuation or a Lump Sum?
Most employers will never offer you a lump sum, and here is why. If the lump sum severance is tied to some kind of continuing obligation, confidentiality, one-year non-solicit, or a one-year non-compete, they are never going to give you a lump sum. What would be your incentive for adhering to the non-compete (other than them suing you, of course)? This is why all employers condition severance on some obligation. They will hold you accountable if you violate the terms of those post-employment restrictions by cancelling your severance payments.

At What Level Is Severance Typical?
It varies by industry, but severance is typically only available at or above the director level. Some larger companies offer a severance pay plan to employees at manager levels or above, but they are much rarer these days.

What Are Typical Severance Levels?
Generally speaking, severance ranges for a VP are three to six months, an SVP six to nine months, and C-suite twelve months. **Change of control** provisions typically move that range upwards.

Beware of some typical severance tricks as well. Some employers will deny employees bonuses as part of the severance package. Look out for provisions that say something like, "You must be employed on the date the bonus is *paid* in order to earn it." Well, we all know how that game works, right? Bonuses are not paid until the year following the year of completion, which is usually by March 15 of that following year. Not in the year you actually earned the bonus.

If you do not do anything to change or tweak or modify that provision, an employer can fire you on December 31 and deprive you of the bonus you earned by working the whole year. If your severance does not include the bonus payment for the prior year worked or a pro-rated bonus for the year in which you lose your job, you can be assured that an employer is not going to pay it. Similarly, some employers condition severance on more than just being let go, such as requiring the company to be sold or acquired first (known as a double-trigger provision) and only if you stick around until that happens, which may not be in your best interest.

Include Good Reason Clauses

Good Reason clauses are one of the most sought-after provisions and are typically only available in negotiations for executives at a senior vice president level or higher. During your employment, a Good Reason clause gives you the right to trigger severance if your employer acts against you in a way that impacts your career. These acts include changing your title or reporting line, reducing your role or responsibilities, lowering your salary or bonus, or forcing you to change where you live to accommodate the business. Such provision gives you enormous leverage when paired with a significant severance allowance. The Good Reason clause essentially says to an employer, "If you reduce my duties and title and my responsibilities, you tell me that the company is forcing me to relocate from Georgia to Washington, D.C., or you otherwise materially breach your obligations to me like not paying me my salary or not setting my target bonus, then I get to trigger my severance the same way that you would trigger the severance if you fire me without cause."

Good Reason is basically your power to terminate the relationship on your own terms.

With this clause in your employment agreement, you can hold your employer accountable for their most important obligations to you. They know that if they fail to do so, you will walk out the door with a payout they did not want to make that will effectively serve as a signing bonus for your next job. That is what leverage truly looks like.

Negotiate Equity Acceleration

The average tenure of an employee at any given employer is four years. One of the reasons why four years became the average tenure is because employer stock options typically vest over a four-year period. This is why motivated career professionals do not accept stock options with longer vesting periods: they know that they can do better with a new employer after four years or that it is too risky to expect an employer to keep them employed for more than four years and therefore they could forfeit options with a longer vesting period.

There are methods, however, of getting that equity package to vest in a shorter period than four years. This is known as **equity acceleration**, and it gives you some protection against involuntary termination. You can bargain with your employer to start the vesting immediately rather than waiting up to a year for the first set of options to vest. You can also request that some or all of that four-year vesting package instantly vest if you are terminated in connection with your employer being sold or acquired (which we previously covered as **change of control**). This will operate as another basis to give the employer pause before terminating your employment.

Alternatively, if you receive an extended notice period as discussed above, that notice will also bridge vesting of equity. For example, if you receive a sixty-day notice period and the company terminates your employment on March 1 but your next vesting period is not until May 1, the extended notice period will allow you to capture the equity vesting on May 1.

Insist on some of these impactful changes to your employment terms. Hoping for better is not a strategy!

CHAPTER NINE

CAN YOU NEGOTIATE YOUR OWN DEPARTURE WITH SEVERANCE?

"You miss 100 percent of the shots you don't take."
Wayne Gretzky

In the last chapter, we talked about negotiating provisions to protect professionals from involuntary termination. But what if you never negotiated any of these provisions as part of your employment relationship and know you are about to be laid off or fired? Or what if you feel so distraught or out of alignment with your position that you do not believe you have any choice but to walk out without a job waiting for you?

Just giving up and turning in your laptop to HR is the very last thing you should ever do. That emotional, reactive, or impulsive behavior is the opposite of the appropriate action, because there are still alternatives to giving up. We think we are somehow sending a message in our dramatic departure, but in fact, we are leaving money on the table and harming our careers and reputations.

Walking away from a position can have profound consequences, particularly if you are not walking into a new company. Leaving aside the obvious – you have no income once you walk out the door and unemployment being a poor substitute for salaried work – you may still have post-employment restrictions like non-competes or bonus clawbacks and forfeiture, and all you are doing is locking in terrible losses. What you are experiencing here is like selling your house for less than the outstanding mortgage you owe. You cannot afford to make that mistake.

There is a completely different way to handle this, but it requires you to take a step back and do the very last thing your employer expects. *Speak your mind*. Positively, assertively, and directly, assert yourself. In a manner framed around your value, share with your employer that they have caused you career derailleur and how you have suffered loss because of misalignment, termination, and so forth.

Lack of Severance Agreement Is Not Fatal to Separation Payments

We often overestimate the level of knowledge management has about the state of careers when in fact, they may simply have no insight into the issues you are facing on the job. Here is a real-world example of this phenomenon: An executive is suddenly let go after only two months in a position and is told it was a "bad fit" by his boss. There is no plausible explanation for the decision other than a difficult and insecure boss who disliked being challenged by the new executive who, responsibly, called attention to problems in the division that his boss managed. His boss became defensive and responded by retaliating against his new subordinate.

This was a devastating end-of-career event for the executive. He endeavored to discuss the matter with HR to no avail. In fact, on the first go around on severance, the company offered a few weeks of pay because it was "sorry" that situation happened. However, sympathy is not synonymous with accountability. Sympathy is an emotion. Accountability is about action, responsibility, and understanding in response to factual information.

In the course of speaking with the executive, it became clear that the executive had failed to properly address with HR the issues he was having with his boss. One letter and two discussions with an attorney later, the executive received more severance than he ever thought possible.

What was the difference? The executive hiring an attorney as a hired gun? Perhaps, but not for the reason you think. The attorney never interacted with the company at all. Instead, he coached the executive on how to reframe the narrative of what he had experienced using detailed, well-organized factual information using language that forced HR to rethink the matter. The approach made all the difference.

Considering the matter in this new light led HR to the right conclusion: the executive's manager had used him as a scapegoat for the problems in his division. It was not that the executive was a bad fit; it was that the manager acted in an immature fashion and did not know how to handle his differences with the employee. HR interviewed the fired employee, better grasped the problem, and offered a separation package reflective of the company's accountability for the situation.

In any separation negotiation, the right approach matters and can often make the difference between two weeks' notice pay and a real separation package.

Resignations Can Come with Payouts

Time and again, employees walk out the door impulsively when they feel disrespected or dishonored. Perhaps because they did not get the job they bargained for or the promotion they thought they deserved. Even those who have built in protections against changes to their position without their consent might feel compelled to walk out rather than stay and fight!

This phenomenon occurs with even greater frequency when professionals *have not* negotiated those protections, such as the aforementioned Good Reason clause. There is a certain logic to that approach. If the employer did not agree to a severance when they hired you, why would they give you anything on departure? Sure, you can threaten them. You can even lawyer up. Prepare for disappointment in that approach, including a long struggle, distraction, damage to your social or home life, and likely dissatisfaction with the outcome.

Before you go down that road, there is another path that is guaranteed to provoke a more positive response than a threat: dialogue with the employer. It is shortsighted to assume there is no one who is prepared to listen to an honest account of why the company should be held accountable for your job situation. Perhaps you worked for a narcissist who sabotaged your career, or your insecure manager painted a false picture of your career. Maybe you were illegally victimized by the business. Never accept that a situation is hopeless until you have exhausted the resources available to you where you work, and of course you have nothing to lose by speaking up for yourself – you are leaving anyway!

Similarly, suppose you have a severance agreement with your employer, but the company has not shown any interest in terminating you despite your desperate need to leave. You cannot quit because you will forfeit the severance that the company offers. In most cases, employers will negotiate a package with you. How is that possible? Why would an employer be willing to pay you? Here are some of the reasons employers will offer packages in exchange for your agreement to separate.

You Have Claims Against the Company
The employer knows you have legitimate legal or business claims against the company, so they are willing to allow you to leave with severance. What they want is a release of your claims against them. Essentially you get paid in exchange for agreeing not to sue them. This is critical, powerful leverage.

Employee's Remorse
You jump into a job and there is a fundamental failure to align. Believe it or not, a number of companies actually hold themselves accountable to employees when mismatches arise. They recognize that dragging out a failed relationship benefits no one and it is best to part with employees amicably and quickly.

Act of God
With greater frequency in recent years, employees have encountered employment situations impacting the value of their positions but entirely outside of their control: a financing failure, a clinical trial that did not work out, or worse, a corporate restructuring. Now, the employer could no longer deliver on the promises made to their employees. Many employers did the right thing in these situations, however. Rather than firing them, the employers agreed to separation packages (even though the employees would otherwise only receive those packages in the event of termination or did not have severance agreements at all.)

So exactly how do you get an employer to offer up a package when they have no legal responsibility to offer it to you? Sometimes holding employers accountable for career derailleur or job loss involves nothing more than the right approach and the right narrative.

What is the right approach? Open with a discussion of your employment situation, what you brought to the table, where the relationship is now, and that it is time to bring it to some kind of resolution beneficial to both parties. It is possible that the employer is unwilling to bargain at the end of a relationship if there was no alignment on severance, but that is not always the case. Either way, negotiating an exit package can be done at the end of a relationship even if it was not agreed upon beforehand.

The right narrative frames the accountability discussion. It consists of assertive communication directed at explaining the nature of the problem and why it has led to an employee's desire to leave with a separation package. The success rate in receiving a package or improving one also depends greatly upon your value to the organization, including what you delivered to the company, the employer's impression of you, and the nature of the issue or grievance giving rise to the current employment situation. The employer's knee jerk reaction will always be that what they have offered is "fair," so an argument based on fairness will not have an impact. An employer often believes they have properly evaluated a severance package for a specific employee by examining these two things:

- Whether a reasonable person in the employee's position would accept the package.
- Whether resolving the claims against the employer would justify giving the employee an enhanced package. (Success rates vary markedly here. In our experience, executives attempting this approach have been successful roughly seventy percent of the time.)

Depending on leverage, you can resign and still get a severance package as a quid pro quo for giving up future litigation rights. Know your rights and options!

CHAPTER TEN

DO CAREER COACHES REALLY MAKE A DIFFERENCE IN EMPLOYMENT OPPORTUNITIES?

*"A good coach can change a game.
A great coach can change a life."*

John Wooden

We saved the biggest error professionals make in their careers for last: You can maximize your chances for a successful employment relationship without a good coach. Ironically, we grow up with coaches for just about everything, including sports, musical instruments, school work, standardized tests, you name it. Anyone who has played an organized sport or hired a personal trainer knows that having a dedicated and knowledgeable coach can make the difference between simply passing the time and reaching – and often exceeding – goals.

So why did we decide that we no longer need coaches in our adult years? Somehow, we think we have all the answers when entering the workforce as a career professional. Or perhaps we do not see the value proposition, maybe because the cost is coming out of our own pockets. We need to drop the excuses. We need coaches even more in our adult years when the stakes are higher and the knowledge gaps are greater. Put simply, coaches can make the difference between greater careers and mediocre ones.

Let us kick off the discussion by identifying what we mean by professional career coaches. Career coaches come in many flavors, including resumé writing, work performance, networking/social media, compensation, career negotiation, and outplacement to name a few. Career coaches are not to be confused with specialized professionals who complete tasks we are unwilling or unable to complete on our own. We have accountants to manage our taxes. We use lawyers to manage our legal issues. But career coaches are something else entirely. Career coaches do not fix things *for* us; they work *with* us to motivate and help us achieve our potential.

Rebecca Weaver, Founder of HRuprise, an employee advocacy and HR consulting firm, put it this way: "A great career coach helps you see beyond your current role and helps you be the architect of your career. They will push you outside of your comfort zone, because that's where growth happens."

Career coaches should not be found in the workplace. You may have mentors at work or confidantes that help you better understand your employer or a particular matter. While these individuals are incredibly important in educating you about matters on the job, they cannot help you manage your career. They are often not trained in performance management and, therefore, do not understand what you need in terms of career development. They may also be limited in their ability to deliver the kind of objective career advice that you need to hear – but may not necessarily want to accept – about yourself or your career path or track at work. They may also have a divided sense of priorities given that your employer is paying their bill.

Imagine if hiring a career coach could be the difference between accepting what is offered at face value or considerably increasing your income. What if you could gain stock options and hidden benefits and experience greater financial freedom? What if you could adapt measures to shift your thinking at work in order to increase your success, build more opportunities, and develop more confidence in yourself in the process? Career coaches are the secret weapon to maintaining trajectory. They are also cost affordable, particularly if they can either save you money by helping you reposition yourself or help you make more money and gain a greater package.

So why don't more people hire career coaches?

The feedback we have received from professionals at almost every career level is that they have not hired career coaches in the past because they believe they have (or should have) all the answers and are content to go it alone. Perhaps they do not see the benefit in spending money now, particularly if they are in between positions and money is tight. Ironically, they view hiring those other types of coaches as a necessity. It is time to start thinking of career coaches the exact same way – as a necessity.

Bobby Knight, one of the most celebrated coaches in college basketball, once said, "The will to succeed is important, but what's more important is *the will to prepare.*"

You are your greatest long-term investment and the most important asset in your life. Investing in someone who can help protect and grow the value of that asset over the length of your career is a critical aspect of sustained career growth and development.

There are career coaches for every area of expertise. To maximize success, find someone trained and experienced in handling your particular coaching needs to help you. Here are just a few specific ways that coaches can assist you.

Repositioning

Coaches who specialize in executive placement or outplacement offer an array of services that assist in career transition and rebuilding. Resumé writers and recruiters fall into this category, as well. Sometimes the only thing that distinguishes employment negotiations is the skill of the coach that empowers *you* to land a better opportunity or pivot within your current organization.

Knowledge

There is an enormous amount of information unknown to professionals about the negotiation process, including how to handle the verbal negotiation stage and the written one. Both must be carefully assessed and evaluated before an offer is accepted. The knowledge gap is steep, and the information is critical to success. Remember, coaches do this for a living and handle matters like this every day. You handle these issues every few years. Benefit from their up-to-date knowledge of industry practices.

Time

Professionals do not have the luxury of unlimited time while evaluating new opportunities. In most cases, employers will expect feedback on verbal and written offers within 24 to 72 hours, sometimes shorter and frequently over a weekend. This could be because of the immediate needs of the role, the fact that they have other candidates waiting in the wings, or that they just want to lock you up quickly before you accept a competing offer. Regardless, time is not on your side. Having someone capable of assisting you in the offer review and negotiation process is a pivotal aspect of success. Good career coaches can boost the value of a position considerably.

Perspective and Objectivity

As the saying goes, we do not have the ability to serve as our own coaches. That perspective eludes us because it is so difficult to maintain. Objective perspective is the key to successful career negotiations by training professionals who can see the issues associated with an employment relationship that we cannot readily observe ourselves. This is also why our spouses and loved ones make for poor coaches. They tend to be biased, or at least not objective, often lack industry expertise, and, quite frankly, may not be completely honest with you about your blind spots or faults.

Bill Cordivari held many executive positions for over thirty years and was a company president at Johnson & Johnson. He is now a business leadership coach and shares this personal perspective with his clients:

> Michelangelo's six-ton sculpture of David is considered one of the greatest works of art of all time. Legend has it that when Michelangelo was asked how he created such a masterpiece, he replied, "I created nothing. David was always there in the block of marble before I started. I just chipped away all of the excess."

> Most executives and other motivated career professionals can also be masterpieces if they work with an experienced coach who can help them remove the excesses of self-defeating behaviors and limited thinking that holds them back. Also, an experienced coach is one of the few people you can trust for the necessary feedback you need to hear – with no side agendas, other than helping the executive become their best.

Preventative Maintenance

We all have inherent blind spots. Hiring a coach is much like doing preventative maintenance on your car or home. It is easier to catch issues on the front end before they become larger problems down the road. Remember the discussion earlier about the decay rate and how circumstances can radically accelerate decay? Effective coaches can reduce or eliminate decay. Again, it is all about shifting mindsets and perspectives. Career coaches will help you figure out the issues that are holding you back and impeding performance, help you crystallize and organize your thoughts and approaches at work, and help manage the difficult challenges in performance you may often tackle alone because you do not believe anyone can help you confront them. They can also help you realize when it is time to move on from a current position because of how unhealthy the work situation has become.

Confidentiality

We are frequently asked about using coaches provided directly by employers. These coaches can certainly be of some benefit. But for whom does the coach really work? Can you trust their guidance implicitly? Do you expect them to maintain strict confidentiality, and do they agree with your expectations? These are all unknowns at best and pitfalls at worst. However, career coaches hired directly by you work only to serve your interest and should agree to absolute confidentiality with any problem you bring to their attention. They have no allegiance to anyone but you. In almost every employment situation, the first step you should take to resolving problems should be consulting an outside coach. An outside, unbiased source can serve as a completely confidential sounding board – nothing will get back to your employer.

All world-class athletes and C-suite execs have coaches! The right coach has specific expertise and a broad perspective that will provide you with an unbiased assessment of your situation.

CONCLUSION

THE IMPORTANCE OF NAVIGATING YOUR CAREER

"The only way to do great work is to love what you do.
If you haven't found it yet, keep looking.
Don't settle."

Steve Jobs

The insights we have shared in this book represent decades of professional work and evolving thought leadership in improving and enhancing career journeys for motivated career professionals. Debunking some of the misconceptions and mindset shifts of how to negotiate employment arrangements will close the knowledge gap. However, professionals require a more precise set of tools to solve the problems they face in various circumstances of negotiation. We searched in vain for these resources but to no avail. So, we decided to create our own. For years, career professionals have struggled to find trusted, reliable resources in response to a hiring process controlled almost exclusively by the employer. Sure, if you are fortunate enough to have the right mentor, you might be able to get the support you need. You might know an employment attorney knowledgeable about reviewing job offers who also has availability in the narrow window you have to respond to your offer. This leaves a lot to chance. But it can be a true hit-or-miss process. So, we thought to ourselves, *what if we could create a tool for the entire process, start to finish? One that brings analysis, intelligence, and support to professionals at varying levels of their career journeys. A personalized process tailored to the unique issues confronting professionals that provides instantaneous results. One that also gives them confidence that they are getting the right advice for their careers.*

So, we created NAV™.

NAV offers a cutting-edge, world-first system combining under one roof three unique assessment tools: analysis through artificial intelligence, detailed reporting, and coaching. Our reverse artificial intelligence thinks the way a human coach does in assessing current and prospective opportunities, not to predict results but to *recommend* them. Reporting like a credit score comparing your two opportunities. Coaching through your own dedicated team of career coaches knowledgeable about your challenges and how to get you where you need to go.

Armed with these powerful tools, you can finally get the answers you need for the career you deserve. Better assessment of the value remaining in your current position and how much better a new position might possibly be. Truly, your compass to a better career.

We proudly invite you to explore NAV. If you use the QR code listed on the back of this book, you will gain access to our system at navscoring.com and begin improving your career trajectory immediately.

CAREER EXERCISES

CAREER EXERCISES

EXERCISE ONE
MAP YOUR CAREER TO FRAME YOUR LEVERAGE

It is helpful to see where you are, where you have been, and where you want to be. You have no doubt made incredible strides over the course of your career trajectory. Take a few minutes to map out your career trajectory from inception. You are where you are right now because your career has evolved over time. So, take a self-assessment of your career, your accomplishments (including the highs and lows), and your goals to evaluate both the growth as well as areas for improvement.

As you list each position, consider the following:

- The current value of the position to you.
- The remaining value of the position.
- The value you bring to the position.

If you are listing previous positions, evaluate them according to what you believed to be true at the time.

These data points will allow you to understand where you are in your career and help you plot the next stage in your trajectory. As you list each position, try to remember what the plan was for you in this role. Then compare that place to where you are now. Have you achieved the desired outcome? If not, is it attainable? Now you can begin to properly understand the issue at hand and the actions to take to reach your desired results. It is incredibly valuable to note where you are, where you are going, and where you want to be when you are ready.

Position 1:

a. The value the position held for you when you accepted the position
b. The value you brought to the position
c. The value you got out of the position
d. The circumstances that led to you leaving the position

Plan or Growth Achieved in the Role:

Position 2:

a. The value the position held for you when you accepted the job
b. The value you brought to the position
c. How the position was as expected or varied from your previous position
d. The value you got out of the position
e. The circumstances that led to you leaving the position

Plan or Growth Achieved in the Role:

(Repeat Until Current Position)

Current Position:

a. The current value of the position (using the above points as a guide)
b. The remaining value of the position
c. Are your personal goals for your career accomplished by remaining in this position or with this particular employer? Why do you believe that to be the case?
d. Honest assessment of whether those goals (and your personal value) are better served by leaving your current position or this particular employer
e. Have you considered whether there are other opportunities or positions that might benefit or advance your career trajectory more than your current position? If you believe that to be the case, begin researching those opportunities

EXERCISE TWO

WHAT TO FOCUS ON WHEN DECIDING WHETHER TO MOVE POSITIONS INTERNALLY OR EXTERNALLY

1. What will the new position do to advance your **span of authority and control**, future career, skill set, and knowledge?

2. How much time will you need to invest in the new position to be successful?

3. What does your advancement look like in your current job situation vs. what you can achieve elsewhere?

4. How will changing supervisors impact your development?

5. How long has your supervisor been in the role? Do you get a sense that this supervisor is getting ready for promotion (allowing upward movement) or just settling in?

6. How does the new position meet your career expectations and advance them?

7. What is the purpose of your new position from the employer's perspective?

8. What is the business problem that is being solved by hiring you for the role?

9. How critical is the position to the employer?

10. What considerations do you need for work flexibility? Will you be on call 24/7 and need to work weekends or have a reasonable steady-state schedule?

11. What is your operational support?

12. Where do you fit on the organizational chart?

13. What mentoring is available?

14. When will you be eligible for promotion?

15. What is the future career path for your role?

16. What leadership or training programs are available?

17. How are you going to be introduced to the business?

18. What will your new coworkers think of you joining the team, or will current coworkers resent you for being moved into a new role?

19. What happened to the last person in your role?

20. How often are salary and performance reviews conducted by the employer?

21. Was there an internal search for candidates? Why didn't it work out?

22. If the role is newly created, what has the company done to set it up for success? Is there enough work to justify the role?

23. Is there a clear reporting line?

24. Is there any commitment to remote work, and is it captured in the agreement? If so, are there built-in opportunities for team building? What are the expectations for facetime in the office?

EXERCISE THREE

DUE DILIGENCE REGARDING YOUR INTERVIEWS AND ANALYSIS

This exercise helps you in vetting your prospective employer before the negotiations stage. Approach the matter the way you might if you were buying the company hiring you. Where would you go in the search, and what would you ask? In any merger or acquisition, you would engage in due diligence. So why not do the same here? Make a due diligence plan and find a coach to help you understand the information you gather.

Start with the **Securities and Exchange Commission (SEC)**. For publicly traded companies, you can research a company simply by plugging the company name into the Electronic Data Gathering, Analysis, and Retrieval System (EDGAR) at www.sec.gov. All public companies use EDGAR to file their required documentation with the SEC, so it is a robust resource for research. The online filings provide the latest information about a prospective employer's financial performance, operations, lawsuits, and shareholder disputes. Additionally, employment offers and agreements for the C-suite leaders of the company can be found here! The **Form 10-K** is the first place you should look when beginning your research. It contains some of the most comprehensive information available to investors about a given business.

Financial information about private companies is more challenging to obtain. You must be tactical in your inquiries through indirect methods. For example, if you are entitled to equity, you can request a copy of the company's capitalization table, which is a breakdown of all the equity held by the company shareholders. Then request the last valuation study the company conducted, which is called a **409A valuation**. You can also ask the company what its market cap is currently and what its current and projected revenue forecasts are.

And here are some questions to ask or develop an understanding of while you are interviewing with them:

1. Are there any financial issues known by the company that would impact the long-term viability of my position?

2. What is the reputation of the business? What does my network say about the culture of the organization?

3. How does the company maintain its core values?

4. Are there plans to take the company public? If so, what is the timeline?

5. What has attrition been like in this department, group, and the company overall?

6. When was the last time the company conducted an across-the-board salary review or adjustment? Is a cost-of-living adjustment (COLA) standard practice?

7. If applicable, what funding round is the company on, and when will it be going for its next funding opportunity? How are my equity options being valued if I am eligible to receive them?

8. Have there been any significant issues with morale or complaints raised against the company or within my department about employee treatment or the work environment?

GLOSSARY

409A valuation (Exercise 3)
Report by an independent third party that assesses the estimated fair market value of a company's common stock. All 409A valuations should be reviewed with an attorney given that companies at every stage are valued differently, particularly if the company has limited market value.

At-will employment (Chapter 2)
A term of art meaning that you and your employer have the right to terminate the employment relationship at any time and for any lawful reason.

Benefits (Chapter 4)
Typically intangible perks or forms of compensation that have a cash value, including vacation, health care, expense allowances for travel and entertainment, car allowances, gym memberships, and so forth.

Change of control (Chapter 8)
The specific circumstances that trigger a change of ownership of the company. Change of control definitions vary from company to company, although triggers can be similar. Some common triggers for change of control include: (a) the sale of all or substantially all of a subject company's assets; (b) any merger of the subject company with another company; (c) the transfer of a certain percentage of the subject company's issued and outstanding shares to an acquiring entity; and (d) transactions in which more than 50 percent

of the board members change or a change in shareholders who have the right to elect more than 50 percent of the board. Many change of control provisions have exceptions built into their definition as well.

Cost-of-Living Adjustment (COLA) (Chapter 6)
An increase in salary or benefits to address inflation calculated annually using the Consumer Price Index for Urban Wage Earners and Clerical Workers (CPI-W).

Depreciation (Chapter 6)
An accounting method allocating the cost of an asset (like a car) over its useful lifespan.

Diminishing returns (Chapter 6)
An economic principle that refers to the reduction in the rate of profit from an investment as the investment in a given area increases but where other variables relating to the investment remain at a constant or steady state.

Equity acceleration (Chapter 8)
A term of art meaning that the vesting of the stock over time actually happens more rapidly than your vesting schedule ordinarily allows. For example, if you have a vesting schedule of four years before all of the stock is exercised and acceleration occurs, most, if not all, of the stock becomes automatically capable of being exercised.

Fixed compensation (Chapter 4)
Objective cash-based compensation not tied to performance, such as annual salary, sign-on bonuses, relocation packages, and other bonuses not based on a target.

Glossary

Form 10-K (Exercise 3)

The form submitted by publicly traded companies to file an annual report with the SEC. The annual report provides extensive information on a comprehensive overview of the company's business and financial condition and includes audited financial statements.

Good Reason (Exercise 3)

A clause contained in senior-level employment agreements, typically SVP or higher. Good Reason clauses run parallel to the employer's ability to terminate employment without cause. They enable employees to resign with severance and other benefits if those are offered in the event the company terminates employees without cause where the employer takes action in violation of the employment agreement, changes title or duties and responsibilities, requires relocation as a condition of employment after the job starts, reduces salary or target benefit, and so forth. Good Reason clauses vary from company to company, although certain terms have become standard by industry.

Job title (Chapter 4)

The formal expression or designation by the company of the function an employee serves within an organization. Job titles can mean very different things internally and externally to a business. Where possible, job titles should express seniority level in a universally accepted way (e.g., director, officer, or C-suite) and be descriptive of the actual work you do (e.g., marketing or clinical studies) rather than generic or ambiguous titles such as "head" or "lead."

Notice period (Chapter 2)

The time period that an employer or employee offers the other party after they give notice where they remain employed during the period in question.

Onboarding (Chapter 6)

The process of integrating new employees into a company. Onboarding typically includes assistance in transitioning into a new role, such as training on company or business functions.

Opportunity cost (Chapter 4)

The costs or risks of forfeiture inherent in an existing position or taking a new position, such as clawback of a sign-on bonus for resigning or post-employment restrictions.

Position description (Chapter 3)

A detailed statement of the nature of a position and the duties and responsibilities associated with it. Position descriptions are critical to framing mutual expectations about the position you have been hired to fulfill for an employer.

Post-employment restrictions (Chapter 7)

Certain policies or agreements requested by an employer that impose certain legal rights or requirements on an employee during and after your employment, such as confidentiality, return of property on termination, and competing against employers or trying to hire employees away after you leave employment.

Reporting line (Chapter 3)

Defines and designates the relationship between an employee and those to whom they have responsibility. There are two kinds of reporting lines – solid-line, which relates to your direct reporting into a supervisor or manager; and dotted-line, which relates to your indirect reporting to someone else within the organization that may have input into your duties and responsibilities. Reporting line is another critical area for clarity and definition because it communicates the significance of your role or level and who will be responsible for your growth, development, and performance.

Retention (Chapter 6)
Describes the rate at which employers are capable of keeping productive employees and reducing turnover. We prefer to think of it as the active involvement of both you and your employer to demonstrate an interest in your continued employment with the organization.

Return on investment (ROI) (Chapter 6)
The measure of the profitability of an investment reflected in a percentage derived by dividing the amount earned from an investment minus the present value of the investment by the cost of the investment and multiplying that amount by 100. For example, if you exercise 100 shares of company stock at $100 per share and the stock rises to $1000 per share, the ROI is 900 percent ($100,000-10,000/10,000 x 100).

Salary band (Chapter 4)
The pay range established by a company for given roles based on market conditions and internal value.

Securities and Exchange Commission (SEC) (Exercise 3)
The federal government agency in charge of the nation's securities industry. The SEC was launched following the stock market crash of 1929 as part of the Securities Exchange Act of 1934, which was designed to bolster confidence in capital markets.

Severance (Chapter 2)
The compensation and/or benefits an employer provides to an employee in connection with termination of employment.

Span of authority and control (Chapter 4)
The number of direct reports or subordinates you have under authority, supervision, or your reporting line.

Variable compensation (Chapter 4)
Performance-related compensation, such as target bonuses, commission, equity in the form of stock options or restricted stock, long-term incentive plans, bonus pools, or what is known as phantom or synthetic equity (a payout only on sale or company exit).

ACKNOWLEDGEMENT

We need to take a moment to recognize the people who have supported, encouraged and inspired us on this journey.

To Christina and Jack Rooze (Heather's parents), your boundless encouragement and never-ending support allowed us to achieve this goal. You modeled so many of the concepts of tenacity and goal setting within this book and you have been amazing role models. This book was written because of the opportunities you helped to create and we are eternally grateful.

To Bobbi and Jack Matalon, we thank you for always loving us, believing in us and supporting our dreams. Your passion for family has helped shape us and the next generation of our family.

To our daughters, Olivia, Julia, Abigail and Isabelle, thank you for your enthusiasm, insightful (and often amusing) anecdotes and support that kept us going when life got crazy. You each bring love and levity to our lives and words cannot express how proud we are of each of you. We wrote this book to empower you. Thank you for being our inspiration and motivation to create lasting change where we can.

To our family and friends who have become our family (you know who you are. You are our inspiration and reason for driving change. Thank you for sharing your perspectives and for trusting us with your stories.

Acknowledgement

To our dedicated team of advisors (Simon Pearce, Mark Ciapka, Bill Cordivari, and Michael Pearce), amazing investors, and our charter members: You believed in our dream when we were still trying to formulate our strategy. You asked the hard questions, celebrated the small victories along the way and are the backbone of this publication as well as a driving force behind the realization of our endeavor.

We would also like to thank our incredible marketing (Hunterblu Media), public relations (LBR/PR) and book editing teams (Alice Johnson, Cup O' Content, Rose Boettinger, Lieve Maas) for ensuring that our message was clear, concise and approachable.

Finally, thank you to OlenderFeldman LLP, who stands behind the mission as well as the message of this book and has encouraged and supported us unwaveringly.

AUTHOR BIOS

HOWARD MATALON

Howard Matalon is an equity partner of OlenderFeldman LLP in charge of the firm's Employment Practices and Litigation Group. Howard is an accomplished legal advisor with thirty years of experience offering precision guidance and cost-effective solutions in human capital management to employers and executives alike in a cutting-edge "360-degree" practice across the United States. He previously developed a proactive approach to employment law challenges for employers based on a sophisticated audit and guidance system that manages issues in every stage of the employee life cycle, including hiring, onboarding, retention, and termination.

Howard routinely counsels his clients on a wide range of complex employment issues, including hiring practices and business accountability for workplace conditions and adverse employment actions. He received a Professional in Human Resources® (PHR®) certification from the HR Certification Institute (HRCI). Howard also coaches select executives in their hiring and separation negotiations, the vast majority of whom are women. In 2019, Howard was featured in "Senior Gigs And The Fine Print That Comes With Them," a Forbes article that addressed this topic. Howard utilizes the principles in *Leadership and Self-Deception*, a book developed by the Arbinger Institute, in every facet of his legal and coaching work.

Howard received his Bachelor of Arts from Brandeis University and his JD from Boston University Law School.

HEATHER MATALON

Over the last two decades, Heather's career has spanned consumer marketing, corporate communications, and information technologies at major corporations where she made it a point to concentrate on the "little guy," a decision that allowed her to make a big impact on smaller and lesser-known businesses and brands. She remained steadfastly committed to small businesses as she moved on from the corporate world to more entrepreneurial companies later in her career, and as result, she was called on to testify before Congress in Washington, D.C., as a subject matter expert for the Committee on Small Business and Entrepreneurship.

Heather's focus has always been on lifting up and supporting others. Whether that meant leading women's affiliate groups within major multi-national organizations or mentoring her team and coworkers, helping others succeed has always been Heather's mission. This passion is what led her to develop and cofound NAV™ as a way to empower high-performing employees, particularly women, with the tools and education they need to make strategic and informed decisions about their next career moves.

Heather received her Bachelor of Arts from Vanderbilt University and her MBA from Cornell Johnson Graduate School of Management. Heather lives in Far Hills, New Jersey, with her husband Howard and their four adventurous daughters.

Made in the USA
Middletown, DE
12 March 2025